" Ground Cover !
Please use ↑ !
Maybe first Week .... ,
I Week prior

SECOND EDITION

START YOUR OWN

BACKYARD PLANT NURSERY

CRAIG WALLIN

**Start Your Own
Backyard Plant Nursery**

Dedication

If you've been downsized, outsourced, grown tired of the rat race or just need more income and a brighter future, this book is for you. If you're ready to take charge and become your own boss, this book is for you.

Since the first edition of this guide was published several years ago, I've heard from dozens of readers who have started their own profitable local plant nurseries. I'm thankful they have shared their stories, because their contributions have made this second edition a bigger, better and more useful guide.

And a special thanks to all the other established growers and nursery owners who have contributed their tips, wisdom and knowledge to make this edition even better.

Thanks for buying this guidebook and may your new nursery business thrive and prosper!

Craig Wallin

Table of Contents

Introduction

Starting a backyard plant nursery can be a wonderful way to turn your love of plants and gardening into cash. It's one of the best ways to "bootstrap" a few hundred dollars into a good income.

When people think of a plant nursery, the local garden center usually comes to mind. Fact is, most garden centers produce very few of the plants they sell. Instead, they purchase their plants from specialty nurseries that actually grow the plants.

You'll find specialty nurseries ranging in size from small backyard nurseries to giant regional wholesale nurseries, who might supply retailers in several states. That's the beauty of the plant nursery business – there's room for everyone, from "mom & pop" part-timers to multi-million-dollar corporations. And it might surprise you to find out how many of the corporate giants got started as backyard growers with little more than a shovel and a wheelbarrow.

The secret to making good money with a backyard plant nursery is to specialize in plants that are in demand, and can be container grown to save space, water, time and labor.

Growers who live in a small town or rural area can also make a good income focusing on wholesale plant sales to retail nurseries and landscapers around their region. One local grower who specializes in ornamental grasses sells her entire year's production to retail garden centers in a city an hour's drive away.

One of the best advantages of having your own plant nursery is being able to buy wholesale at deep discounts. There are hundreds of wholesale nurseries that specialize in what are called in the nursery trade "plugs, liners & whips", which are different types of plant starts. All you'll need to do is re-plant them in a larger pot and wait a year or so for the plants to grow to saleable size. The profit margins are amazing. You'll find plant starts for 25 cents that can be resold in a year for $5 – a 2,000 percent mark-up.

Once you've got your "mother" plants, you can easily propagate more by cuttings or root division and reduce your plant costs to zero. This can really make a difference with ground covers and ornamental grasses, for example, because most buyers need dozens of plants, not just a few.

Are you a self-starter?

When you start your own nursery business, it's up to you to make things happen. There is no boss to turn to - it's just you and another ten flats of seedlings to re-pot or mix another pile of potting soil. From scheduling to organizing, you're in charge, and the work won't get done until you dig in and do it! Again, the rewards are great, especially when you hear from an appreciative customer who is grateful for the beautiful plants you grow.

> *"If you really want to do something, you'll find a way.*
> *If you don't, you'll find an excuse."*

JIM ROHN

How To Use This Book

I'm proud of you! You're doing something that most of us only dream about but never begin - starting your own business. There are many steps that go into starting a business, and it can seem like an impossible task. Where do I start? What should I do first? Who can I turn to for help? Now, with this step-by-step guide you will have the help you need to start your own successful and profitable backyard plant nursery.

You should plan to follow the startup steps listed in the guide to get your new nursery well underway in about a month. Once you've got all the basics in place, you can actually start growing plants for profit.

If you think 30 days is not enough time, just remember Mark Zuckerberg wrote the first version of Facebook in just 30 days! So what are you waiting for? Let's get started.

CHAPTER 1

What Type of Plant Nursery Is Best?

To ensure that your new backyard plant nursery is successful, you'll need to consider all the factors that will affect your new business before you start. To help you, here's a checklist of questions you'll need to ask about your new nursery:

Plant nurseries fall into two basic types – wholesale and retail. Wholesale plant nurseries grow plants to sell to other nurseries, landscapers and retailers, such as garden centers. Retail nurseries typically grow plants for retail sale to homeowners and landscapers.

If you already have a location, that may be a factor in what type of nursery you choose. For example, local ordinances or zoning may prohibit a retail operation, or you may be located in such a remote area that retail customers would have difficulty finding or getting to your location. In addition, many growers prefer plants to people, and dislike the effort and time it takes to deal with retail customers. Gardeners are great folks, but they love to chat about plants, or get free advice, which can really take a bite out of your workday.

Another factor in choosing the nursery format that's best for you is the type of plants you want to grow. For example, if you're passionate about groundcovers as a specialty crop, your nursery would need to be near a city for retail sales to homeowners and landscapers. Otherwise, wholesaling your groundcovers would be the best way for you to sell a large enough volume of plants to make a good living.

Will the Nursery Site Be Suitable?

1. What was the previous use of the land?
2. Has the land ever been contaminated by pesticides or other toxic chemicals that could still be present in the soil?
3. How is the drainage on the land? A slight slope is best for good drainage.
4. Is the soil suitable for a plant nursery? Hardpan, rocky or heavy clay soils can make it very challenging to grow plants, but container growing can minimize this challenge.
5. Is the land in a flood zone?

Will You Have Sufficient Water?

Growing plants require lots of water, so you'll need to make sure you have an adequate supply for the size of nursery you have planned. Because young plants can be sensitive to minerals in the water, it's advisable to have your water source tested. Most nursery experts agree that "total soluble salts" should not exceed 500 ppm, with less that 200 ppm best. Water sodium levels should not exceed 20-30 percent of total salts. Your local extension agent or soil conservation service office can help you locate a testing laboratory.

An on-site pond is a good source of water for a nursery, with a drilled well a close second. If your well produces a low but steady flow, consider creating a pond on your property to be filled by the well during off-peak times. Newer high-tech liner materials have made the cost of creating even larger ponds quite affordable. For free planning information on building your own pond, visit: www.everliner.com.

How Much Space Will You Need?

Your profits will depend on having the space to grow enough plants to make your nursery profitable. If you stick to container growing, most of your plants will be sold in #1 (one gallon), #2 (two gallon), #5 (five gallon) and #15 (fifteen gallon) sizes. Here's how many of each will fit into a 1,000 square foot area – only 32 by 32 feet, allowing room for paths.

- One-gallon: 3,000 pots per 1,000 square feet.
- Two-gallon: 1,500 pots per 1,000 square feet.
- Five-gallon: 750 pots per 1,000 square feet.
- Fifteen-gallon: 400 pots per square feet.

How Long Before I Can Sell Plants?

If you're growing container plants, the fastest way to get started is to buy starts – also known as plugs or liners, which can be put in one-gallon pots immediately. Most starts are shipped in the spring, so you can pot them, grow them out for a year, then sell them the following spring. Some tree seedlings can be potted early in the spring, then sold later that same year when they have leafed out and the root system has developed. If you start your own plants, add a year to the turn-around time.

Each time you transplant to the next larger pot size, you'll add a year before the plant is ready to sell. If your goal is to start selling plants as soon as possible, buy starts and sell one-gallon pots the next year. Most growers either set aside a portion of their smaller potted plants to repot in larger pots, or simply use their unsold plants to up-size each year. That's one of the benefits of growing landscaping plants. If they don't sell this year, they just keep growing so they're worth a lot more next year!

Trees are slower growing that most other landscaping plants, so you'll need to hold them longer. As a general rule, landscaping trees will grow ½ inch in trunk diameter each year. A tree that you bought as a seedling will take about four years to reach a 2-inch (called "caliper") trunk diameter – a good selling size. Some trees, such as Japanese maples, grow much slower, and can take two to three times as long to reach the same size. But, as you may have noticed, Japanese maples are high priced trees, so you'll be well paid for waiting.

CHAPTER 2

Getting Started

Okay – you've taken care of the preliminary steps: made sure your soil and water supply are suitable, and thought about what you might want to grow and how best to grow your plants. The next step is to do a bit of "market research" before you spend any money on plants and supplies. Don't let the term scare you, market research is just another name for shopping the competition, and asking potential buyers, such as landscapers, what they're buying.

Start by visiting your nearest "Big Box" home center, such as Home Depot or Lowes, to see what they are stocking in their garden center. Pay attention to the sizes being sold. For example, is the Escallonia available in more than one pot size? Is there more than one variety available? Also, make a note of the prices for each size and variety.

If you don't have one of the national home centers nearby, visit your local garden center to see what they're stocking. Check quantities also – if they have three times more barberry than privet, you now know which is the better seller! If an employee wonders why you are taking so many notes, you can either: A. Tell them you're planning a wholesale nursery and want to grow what's in demand. B. Just say that you're working on a landscaping project.

It's also important to keep track of the new varieties being introduced that are not yet widely available in your area. You'll get a better feel for this by checking the web sites of wholesale nurseries who are actively introducing new plants. Commercial rose growers, for example – one of the largest segments of the nursery in dollar volume – never just sell roses, they are always selling new varieties. Most new growers find it easier to start out with a limited number of varieties, specializing in certain plants. For example, you could specialize in container grown hostas, offering twenty to thirty different species both for sale to garden centers and your own retail customers.

Best Sizes to Grow

The smallest size normally used for container growing is the one-gallon (#1) size, or a pot that's about 6" x 6", holding about three quarts of soil. If you plan to sell ground covers in large quantities, a smaller 3" or 4" pot is often used. When you grow the larger plants and shrubs, which will require larger containers, you will usually have much less competition, and the higher prices will more than make up for the extra time required to produce ...ᴄ larger stock.

Many growers choose a mix of smaller plants for the lower priced volume market, and larger plants for the higher prices. Keep in mind that most purchasers associate quality with size, so a well-shaped plant only eight inches tall is not nearly as attractive to them as the same plant twelve inches tall. Each may be the best quality, yet size will make the difference.

Remember that to do the same dollar volume, you'll need to grow many more one-gallon plants for sale than the larger sizes, such as three and five gallons. The small nursery, particularly a retailer, should focus on large quality plants, which are harder to find, and bring top dollar.

Another factor in choosing your sizes is who will be buying your plants. Retail garden centers, for example, have a short season, and prefer to sell small plants that fit in the trunk of a car. Some popular plants for retail garden centers are pines, spruces, yews, junipers, arborvitae and flowering shrubs. If you plan to sell to landscapers, you will find they often want larger plants over a longer season. Many landscaping project designs call for 2"-3" caliper trees, which in a #15 pot can weigh 80 to 100 pounds and require a pickup to haul.

Specialize or Diversify?

You may wish to stay small, specializing in plants that are rare, uncommon or difficult to grow. With thousands of plants to choose from, finding your "niche" in the plant marketplace should not be a problem. Many small specialty nurseries are able to serve a broader regional market this way, focusing on exotica such as Japanese maple or bamboo or cactus.

On the other hand, if you have an acre or less, and want to sell to local retail customers, you should emphasize a diversity of plants. Remember that you will be competing with other retail outlets and should offer your customers something extra to keep them coming back year after year.

The Ten Commandments for a successful plant nursery:

1. Pick your suppliers carefully to insure disease and insect free stock with a high survival rate.

2. Check to ensure that the stock you order will be hardy in your area. Determine the "Plant Hardiness Zone" before you order.

3. Match your planting stock to your planting site. For example, junipers need full sun, yews don't like wet feet, willows do.

4. Plant early. By starting as soon as your land is thawed, the root system can get established before the new upper growth begins. Never allow roots to dry out when planting.

5. Order transplants over seedlings whenever possible. Each time a plant is transplanted, the root system becomes denser and hardier. The extra expense will be repaid in superior plant growth and survival.

6. Allow room for your plants to grow. With adequate spacing, your stock can fill out evenly. No one wants a one-sided plant!

7. Weed your stock. This prevents weeds from choking out lower growth on plants and competing for available water and nutrients.

8. Use time-release fertilizers. The small extra expense will be repaid many times over in higher profits when you sell your larger and healthier plants.

9. Prune often to remove dead growth and encourage new growth.

7. Check your plants often to catch insects and diseases before they get out of control.

CHAPTER 3

Where to Find Suppliers

Other than plant starts, a few hand tools, and a water source, you need only four basic supplies to get started: Containers, fertilizer, labels and soil.

Containers

Plant nurseries use thousands of plastic plant containers, so it's good they are available new at reasonable prices. There are two kinds of basic plastic nursery containers, blow molded and injection molded. Injection molded pots are thicker walled and more durable but cost a bit more than blow molded pots. In addition, used containers can be free, if you know where to look. Any of the distributors listed in the resource section can supply containers in a wide variety of shapes and sizes.

With the prices of new pots so reasonable, does it make sense to try to find free pots? If you're working with an extremely tight budget and are in an area where you can contact landscapers, you should be able to get free pots. Just call a few landscapers and ask them to save their pots for you. In addition, many local recycling centers set aside plastic plant pots for re-use, so check with yours to see what's available. If they're not recycling them now, suggest that they do!

Potting Soil Mix

A good soil mix is essential for growing healthy, quality plants. Two requirements for a good mix are good drainage and the ability to hold moisture. If your mix holds water too long, the plant's roots can become waterlogged. If you're in a rainy area, this becomes even more important. If you're in an area where drought is more of concern, you can add extra peat to the mix to help it hold water longer.

If you're growing in small containers, which dry out faster, more peat is essential also. Adding sand will do the opposite, increasing drainage. Mix a few small test batches, varying the ingredients in each batch, then flood the filled pots with water to see how each blend drains. Pre-mixed potting soil can be purchased from wholesale nursery suppliers in four cubic foot bags, or at most retailers in one cubic foot bags. You'll find the commercial blends are not cheap, because most of them contain a high percentage of peat moss, the most expensive ingredient. To save money on pre-mixed potting soil, wait for a sale, buy broken bags at a discount, or buy in bulk.

Blend Your Own Potting Soil

The alternative to buying pre-mixed potting soil is to blend your own. You'll be able to customize the mix to your climate and plants, as well as save money. Blending the perfect soil mix is like making a pot of soup – each batch is slightly different. Here's a basic formula that can be used "as-is" or adjusted to your specific needs.

1. Six parts topsoil or compost
2. Three parts peat moss
3. Two parts sand

Be sure to check the topsoil or compost for weeds. After you've mixed a batch, check it for good drainage, by filling a pot or two with the blend, and adding water. If water sits on the surface, add sand to improve the drainage.

A small portable cement mixer is ideal for blending potting soil, and much easier on your back. Don't mix too much potting soil, as a little goes a long way with container growing. For example, just one cubic yard will fill 250-300 one-gallon pots. If you're growing groundcovers in the small 3" pots, a cubic yard will fill almost 2,000 pots.

Fertilizing Container Plants

Your goal as a grower is to produce the largest, best-looking healthy plant in the shortest period of time. Controlled-release fertilizers (also called time-release or slow-release) are the best way to achieve that goal. Using regular granular or water-soluble fertilizers can cause problems, such as over-fertilizing or fertilizer burn.

Slow release fertilizers (Osmocote™ is the most widely known brand) are formulated to slowly release nutrients over a longer period of time, rather than all at once. You can choose different formulations, ranging from a 3 to 4 month release period, to 12 to 14 months. This allows you to match the fertilizer closely to the plant you are growing. For example, if you are growing a plant that takes a year to grow out, you simply fertilize once when you pot the plants, with a 12 month formulation, and you're done fertilizing.

The fertilizer has a special coating that controls the fertilizer release to the plant, and because it's coated, it isn't affected by rain or over-watering. Your crop of plants gets a steady diet of nutrients, grows evenly without burning, and produces a healthy plant that your customers love.

Don't buy slow-release fertilizers at your local garden centers, but buy like the pros do, at a wholesale nursery supplier in 50-pound bags. While even the wholesale price may seem high, each one-gallon container plant only needs about a tablespoon, so the cost is very reasonable on a per plant basis.

Most container nursery growers use a slow release fertilizer with a 3:1:2 ratio (nitrogen, phosphorus and potassium), as that ratio is ideal for propagation and continuous feeding of most nursery plants. Blends that include that ratio are the 18-6-12, 19-5-12 and 17-7-12 blends. Your wholesale nursery supplier or the technical representative from the fertilizer company should be able to recommend their best blend for the plants you are growing.

Slow release fertilizers are applied in two ways – by mixing with the soil blend that goes into the plant containers, or by surface application. The advantage of mixing it into the soil blend is that the fertilizer won't spill out if the container tips over or gets blown over.

If you haven't mixed it into the soil, you can add it to the bottom of the planting hole as you are potting up your plants. Putting it in the hole keeps the coating on the fertilizer pellets moister, which allows a more even nutrient release.

As your nursery grows in size, you'll want to add a hand-held fertilizer applicator, set to dispense the exact same amount you set every time you squeeze the trigger. The "Perfect-a- feed" is a popular brand, available at A.M. Leonard.

Although many slow release fertilizers are non-organic, they are quite environmentally friendly, as virtually all the fertilizer is used by the plant, resulting in less nitrate leaching and fertilizer runoff.

Plant Labels

Labeling is essential for container plants. In most areas, it's required by law that any plant sold to the general public be indentified by a label. As a grower, you can add useful information, such as the date the plant was potted, so you know how long it took to mature.

Two types of tags are commonly used, the stake tag that is stuck in the soil next to the plant, and the slip-a-tags that get attached to a branch of the plant. When you're getting started, buy the blank tags and write the plant name and other information on the tag, using an indelible pen. As your nursery grows, you can either use pre-printed labels or print your own.

Growing What Sells

With thousands of profitable plants for the would-be grower to choose from, how do you decide what to grow? Well, despite the belief of many plant lovers that gardening & plant growing is a "higher calling", someone still has to pay the bills and, hopefully, make a profit. The secret to making a profit is to focus on the plant groups that are proven sellers – those that are in demand year after year, by retail customers, the landscapers and the garden center buyers. There are five tried and true types of plants that make sense for the new grower: Landscaping trees and shrubs, ground covers, flowers, herbs and ornamental grasses. In the pages that follow, we'll take a closer look at each of these plant specialties.

CHAPTER 4

Profitable Ground Covers

Ground covers can provide a grower with one of the highest per-square-foot incomes for a plant nursery. The startup costs are modest, and groundcovers are generally easy to grow, easy to market and easy to propagate.

While retail customers will pay a high price per plant for groundcovers, not all growers are fortunate enough to be located near a larger city or town. Most growers are located in remote or hard- to-find spots where land is affordable, and they sell most of their groundcover plants wholesale to retailers and larger landscapers. Don't despair if your location is off the beaten path. You'll still be able to sell groundcovers successfully.

Demand for groundcovers is increasing at a steady clip for several reasons. First, trends. These days, it's become more fashionable to stay home and fix up the house and yard. People are spending more and more to make their homes and yards a refuge from the outside world. The trend trackers call it "cocooning."

There are also practical reasons for the growing popularity of groundcovers.

1. Erosion control. A dense planting of ground covers on a slope can stabilize the soil and keep it from eroding.
2. Weed control. The dense cover provided by many ground covers prevents the weeds from taking over.
3. Reduced watering. A mature planting of a ground cover such as vinca cuts moisture loss, acting as a living mulch to prevent evaporation. This is often a necessity in water-short areas of the country.

In addition, ground covers can provide a solution to two common landscaping problems. When used instead of grass, they can eliminate grass, often paying for themselves in a year or two in reduced maintenance costs. In areas that are too shady for grass, shade loving groundcover such as vinca or winter creeper are a perfect replacement for a lawn. Ground covers also make a great transition planting between lawn and garden or between other large plants.

What is a ground cover? Ask six different gardeners, and you'll likely get six different answers. A basic definition is any plant that creeps, clumps, mats or vines to cover the ground. This definition covers a multitude of plants, from low growing perennials like phlox to herbs like dwarf rosemary to ivies, all those plants that grow close to the ground, spread rapidly and create a dense cover.

Although there are hundreds of plants that are used as groundcovers, we'll focus on just a few, chosen because they are popular, easy to grow and propagate, and reasonably trouble-free for both you, the grower and the consumer who plants them. Don't think you have to grow all of these to succeed as a commercial grower. Many small growers make an excellent living just growing the "Big Four", English Ivy, Pachysandra, Vinca and Winter Creeper.

If you're near a large population center, visit retail nurseries to find out what's popular, and let that guide your choice of plants. Or choose a specialty that appeals to you. One successful grower has a passion for herbs, so her ground cover nursery has row after row of Corsican mint, Lavender, Thyme and other herbs that are wholesaled to retail garden centers.

Recommended Groundcovers

Ajuga. (Bugleweed) This hardy perennial favorite grows fast, with Ajuga reptans (carpet bugle) being the most popular variety. Propagate by root division.

Arctostaphylos. (Bearberry, Kinnikinnick, Manzanita) The preferred species for ground cover use is A.uva-ursi, a sturdy, drought-tolerant plant. Propagate by seed, cuttings or division.

Astilbe. This perennial produces delicate flowers in the spring that are prized for cutting and drying. Propagate by division or start from seed or starts.

Campanula (Bellflower) The Adriatic bellflower, C.garganica is the most popular because of its dense mat of leaves. Propagate by division or start from seeds.

Cotoneaster. The favorite is Creeping cotoneaster, C. adpressus. Another favorite is Rock cotoneaster. Propagate by layering.

Dianthus. (Pinks) This old faithful is widely grown, and can be propagated by cuttings, division or from seed.

Erica. (Heath) This low growing ground cover requires almost no maintenance and is propagated by cuttings or division.

Euonymous (Winter creeper) This popular plant is used where it can grow flat. It sends out fast growing stems that root as they spread. Two popular varieties are Colorata and Radicans. Propagate by cuttings when stems have hardened.

Hedera (Ivy) This hardy evergreen ground cover spreads rapidly and has hundreds of cultivars to choose from. Two varieties of English Ivy (H. helix) are the most popular, "Thorndale and "Baltic." Propagates easily by cuttings.

Hemerocallis. (Daylilly) This plant is easy to grow, easy to maintain and has few pest problems. Propagation by root division every two years.

Hosta. This deciduous perennial is grown mainly for its impressive foliage. Although collectors will pay premium prices for the more exotic cultivars, most growers will be better off producing the more common cultivars. Here are just a few: Albo-marginata, Elegans, Gold standard and H. undulated variegated, better known by the common name, wavy leafed plantain lily. Hostas are propagated by root division in the spring or early fall.

Hypericum. (St. John's Wort) This easy to grow groundcover is widely used where a massed, dense planting is desired, such as erosion control on slopes. It's also used as a medicinal herb. Propagation is by division.

Iberis. (Candytuft) This is a popular ground cover with rock gardeners. Propagate by seeds, cuttings or division.

Liriope. (Lilyturf) Popular varieties include Creeping lilyturf (L. spicata) and Big blue lilyturf (L. muscari). Propagate lilyturf by division.

Lysimachia (Creeping Jenny, Moneywort) This fast-growing creeper is used by landscapers in wet areas, such as around a pond. Propagate by division.

Pachysandra terminalis. (Japanese spurge). This evergreen perennial produces a dark green carpet that thrives in part or deep shade. The underground stems (rhizomes) form a dense mat that's useful for erosion control. Propagate by division or rooted cuttings. Two popular cultivars are "Green carpet" and "Green Sheen."

Parthenocissus quinquefolia. (Virginia creeper) This viney ground-cover is hard to miss in the fall, when the leaves turn bright red. It spreads fast, but will also climb walls, shrubs or trees. Propagate by layering.

Phlox sublata. (Moss phlox, Creeping phlox) A clumping perennial, favored by rock gardeners, with a carpet of solid colors in white, pink or red. Many growers report this is one of their biggest money-makers because of the strong demand. Start with "field clumps" and divide in a year or two to 5-10 more plants, which can then be re-planted. After two years, the divisions will have formed large mats, which can be divided for sale in one-gallon pots.

Potentilla. (Cinquefoil) The most popular variety, Spring cinquefoil (P. verna), provides a low growing dense mat. Propagate by division.

Sedum. (Stonecrop) There are hundreds of species and even more varieties of stonecrop, ranging from one inch dwarfs to two foot tall giants. This plant will grow almost anywhere, and is easily propagated by leaf cuttings.

Veronica. (Speedwell) This classic garden perennial is popular and grows fast. Propagation by division is easy after the plant has flowered.

Vinca minor (Periwinkle) Also known as Myrtle, this hardy, fast spreading ground cover is one of the "big four" of best-selling groundcovers. The easiest way to propagate vinca is by division.

Herbs for Ground Covers

Achillea tormentosa (Wooly yarrow) This evergreen herb spreads far and fast and requires little maintenance. Propagate by seed or division.

Artemesia (Dusty miller, Wormwood) The fine silver-gray foliage makes this perennial herb a popular ground cover for borders. Propagation by division is the quickest method.

Chamomile This evergreen ground cover is widely used in Europe as a lawn substitute, and the flowers make a soothing tea. Propagate by division.

Galium oderatum (Sweet woodruff) This longtime favorite forms a dense mat with underground stems. Propagate by dividing the creeping stems just before it goes dormant in the fall.

Herniaria glabra (Rupturewort) This slow growing herb forms a dark green carpet about three inches high. Propagate by division.

Lavendula augustifolia (English lavender) This ornamental herb has long been grown for its wonderful fragrance and the aromatic oils it produces. Newer dwarf varieties are ideal for ground covers. Propagate by seeds, cuttings or division.

Mentha requienii (Corsican mint) This is the lowest growing mint, topping out at just 1/2", making it a popular groundcover for steppingstone paths. Propagate by division.

Nepeta mussinii (Persian catmint) Cats love this evergreen herb as much as catnip. Humans do too, as it makes an excellent groundcover. Propagate from seeds, root division or runner division.

Rosmarinus officinalis (Dwarf rosemary) This creeping version of the well-known herb makes an excellent groundcover, and you can still snip a sprig or two for your spaghetti sauce! Propagate from seeds or cuttings.

Sagina sublata (Irish moss) Sagina sublata "Aurea" (Scotch moss) Both of these evergreen perennial herbs are widely used between steppingstones and in rock gardens. Propagate by division.

Thymus serpyllum (Creeping thyme) There are several low-growing varieties of this well-known herb that are popular fragrant groundcovers. Other popular varieties include lemon thyme and woolly thyme. Propagate by cuttings or division.

Where to Buy Groundcovers

Once you have a good selection of the groundcovers you've chosen for parent stock growing in your garden, you'll be able to propagate and grow all the new plants you need. Until then, you'll need to purchase your stock. It can be hard to find a local nursery with a complete selection of ground cover varieties, although you should be able to locate the "big four" (English ivy, Pachysandra, Vinca and Winter creeper.) In the resource chapter at the back of this book, you'll find wholesale sources for hundreds of groundcovers.

Ground Cover Propagation

Almost all groundcovers can be easily propagated by division, cuttings or layering. Once you have purchased your initial stock of plants, you can use them as parent stock for new plants to grow and sell. If you're a beginning propagator, purchase a good book or two on plant propagation. You'll find several at Amazon. com . Two of the best are: The Reference Manual of Woody Plant Propagation, and American Horticutural Society Plant Propagation.

Marketing Ground Covers

As a beginning grower, you'll need to study potential markets to determine which ones might be best for you. Also keep up with what other growers are doing, by visiting local garden centers and visiting the web sites of wholesale groundcover growers. This will show you the plants in demand, both locally and nationally. Buyers for plants fall into four categories: direct retail sales, mail order sales, wholesaling plants to garden centers and selling plants to landscapers.

Direct Retail Sales

Selling your plants direct to the retail public will bring the highest profit per plant. Another advantage is that, unlike wholesaling, you'll get paid when you sell the plants, not in a month or two. There are no billing and collection challenges.

Many growers have a "wholesale day" one Saturday morning or two a month during the spring and fall selling season. Run a classified or small display ad in your local paper for the entire week before the sale day. Say "Ground Covers – Wholesale Prices – Public Welcome – 123 Elm Street – Saturday Only 9 a.m. to 3 p.m." As one grower who uses this sales approach said, "Make sure you have some extra sales help, because this one really does work!"

Be sure that the plants are tagged before the day of the sale, so you'll be free to help customers. An effective tagging system uses color-coded tags. Group all your plants into four or five price categories, each with its own color code. A simple sign showing the colors and their corresponding prices is all that's needed.

Be sure to ask plant buyers if they would like to be on your "preferred customer" list for advance notice of future sales or special events. Then, once you've built a mailing list, a postcard mailing to previous customers will let them know about your sales.

Mail Order Sales

Many growers have been successful selling their plants by mail. A specialized category of plants, such as groundcovers, is ideally suited to mail order because potential customers often will be looking for a wider selection than found at their local garden center. This is called "niche" marketing, because it focuses on a narrow category, or niche, in the broader world of plants. You'll need to have a good selection and stock of plants before selling by mail, and put together a small flyer, catalog or web site so prospects can see what you offer.

A small classified ad in national and regional gardening magazines (your local library should have a directory of magazines, or try an internet search), should bring a steady stream of inquiries. Don't charge for your catalog. Why not? Your goal is to get your catalog into the hands of as many prospects as possible, so use the most powerful word in the English language – free. If possible, steer customers to your web site, as you pay nothing for printing or postage, plus they get instant access to your plant list.

Garden Center Sales

If you want to increase your sales volume once you're established and have an ample stock of plants to sell, think about selling wholesale to retail garden centers and retail nurseries. To get started, talk to the owners or managers in your area who might be interested in purchasing your plants. Before you do this, do some comparison shopping to find out what others are charging, both wholesale and retail.

To get started, make up a simple one-page flyer, listing the plants you have for sale, with wholesale prices and terms (terms in the nursery trade are usually "net 30 days"). The advantage of a printed flyer is that the busy owner or manager (this works with landscapers too) is less likely to forget if he has a printed reminder of what you're selling. Another tip – do your selling in the off-season when the buyers have more time to talk to you.

Landscaper Sales

If you live near a larger town or city, chances are excellent that you can sell more plants to landscapers. They usually buy in larger quantities, are repeat customers, and don't require the "hand-holding" that retail customers do. A regular flyer is a good way to keep landscapers up to date on your plant material, pricing and sales. Including tips in the flyer or newsletter on how to use the plants in landscaping projects can increase sales over time.

How to Get Free Advertising

Many counties, tourist offices and local newspapers publish free maps showing all the growers and farms open to the public in their area. Get your nursery on the map, and you could sell plants to many who might never have heard of you otherwise. Grower associations can also be a valuable source of free referrals, especially if you have a growing "niche" such as groundcovers.

Many newspapers do feature stories, large and small, on local businesses. Put together a simple fact sheet on your nursery and take it to your local newspaper. Chances are good you'll get some free publicity.

Be sure to invite local garden clubs to visit your nursery. How about a seasonal flyer offering special discounts just to garden club members? Think about donating plants to your local clubs, schools, churches or other worthy community organizations. They can be used by the group or auctioned off to raise money for their projects. You don't have to give the plants away either. One grower works with his local Master Gardeners, and a church group, who sell his plants at a twice-yearly fundraiser. They keep 40 percent of the proceeds, and he gets "wholesale" prices for his plants. Win – win!

CHAPTER 5

Landscaping Trees and Shrubs

Deep in the Appalachian mountains, Sam Davey, a semi- retired farmer, decided to try growing high-value landscaping plants instead of low-value row crops. Now after just a few years, his six acres contain thousands of azaleas, rhododendrons, Japanese maples, firs, spruce and junipers.

Last year, his stock sold out, without any paid advertising. Most of his plants are sold to local residents, who appreciate quality plants at affordable prices. The rest go to local landscapers and two nearby retail garden centers. As for profits, he will only say that he is making more money than ever before in his life. If he wanted to, he could just grow out his existing stock of seedlings and retire, set for the rest of his life.

Out west, Jack & Karen Cooper have filled their Arizona acre with deciduous trees such as cottonwood, maple and birch. They started with just one cottonwood tree, and from that plant alone have grown and sold thousands of trees. Jack prefers to wholesale his trees to local retail nurseries and landscapers. Most of his trees are sold in 10-gallon pots, which are kept watered with a drip irrigation system. He is able to grow thousands of trees on his acre using this method, and figures he nets about $90,000 per year after expenses.

If you're just starting, it's important to pick plants that are in demand as well as plants that are suited to your area. Because there is such a wide range of climates in North America, you'll need to pay attention to finding the plants that will do well in your area.

Start by taking a pocket notebook to local retail nurseries and jot down what they are stocking in the areas that interest you, such as deciduous trees, evergreen trees and shrubs, flowering shrubs and fruit and nut trees. Make a note of sizes, including the pot size and prices. Pay attention to which plants are stocked in larger quantities – these are usually the best sellers. Nursery trade magazines and web sites- listed in the resource section – are also helpful for learning about plant trends.

Rather than compete head-to-head with the big box stores, or even local garden centers, consider growing unusual and hard-to-get varieties of the same plants they sell, or larger sizes. By offering what customers can't get elsewhere, you'll have a profitable niche and customers will seek you out when they are looking for landscaping plants.

Buying Starter Plants

There are many specialized nurseries that sell only "starter" plants, shrubs, trees and other landscaping plants that are ready to re-pot. Called "liners" or "plugs", these plants are available either bare root or in a plug tray. The advantage of plug trays is that the whole plant, including the root system, can be moved to a larger container with minimal transplant shock.

The resource section at the end of the guide lists many of the larger wholesale nurseries, as well as online directories that will help you find wholesale nurseries in your area. Your state nursery association can locate nearby nurseries that specialize in the plants you are looking for. Whether it's ground covers or evergreens, it's better to buy local, as the varieties offered are likely to be better suited to your climate.

More experienced growers will want to propagate their own plant seedlings by taking cuttings from plants they already have. The advantage of starting your own plants from cuttings is that the cost for plant material is zero, as you already have the mother plant. As most plant starts cost between 50 cents and $1.50 each, you can create a lot of "plant wealth" in just one growing season. For example, if you produce just 1,000 starts a year (most growers can "stick" from 50- 100 cuttings per hour.) you'll save/make up to $1,500, and several thousand when the plants are ready for retail sale.

Most plants are easy to propagate as long as you know when and how to take cuttings. All you need is a good book on propagation, and a misting system to keep the plants moist during the time they are developing a root system. The folks at Dripworks (www.dripworksusa.com) can supply you with all the components of an automatic intermittent misting system, including battery operated timers. For the cost of two or three flats of plugs, you can set up a misting system that will allow you to propagate thousands of plants, and not have to be around to mist them manually.

Re-Potting

Most landscaping trees and shrubs are sold at retail in the larger pot sizes, such as 2,3,5,10 and 15 gallons. Many growers prefer to transplant their seedlings into one-gallon containers first, then re- pot to a larger size as the plant grows. This allows you to sell a plant at an earlier age than if you re- potted the seedling in a larger (5 to 15 gallon) pot.

In the course of your "market research", you may have noticed that the price can double when a plant is sold in a #2 pot instead of a #1 (and triple or better in a #5). For maximum profits, it's best to have a range of sizes as well as varieties. When re-potting, don't forget to add a dose of slow- release fertilizer to the larger pot after you've partially filled it with soil, to insure steady growth and a healthier plant.

If you're going to grow conifers, such as firs and spruce, try to buy transplanted bare-root seedlings labeled as (2-2) or (2-3), as they have a much heavier root system and top growth, and can often be sold at a nice profit in just a year or two. Conifers are slow-growing, and it's better to buy the more mature seedlings than to spend the extra time to do it yourself.

To get a better idea of the re-potting process, let's take a look at one of the most popular nursery trees – Japanese maple (Acer palmatum). While you were doing market research at retail nurseries, you probably noticed several of these trees – at prices from $40 to $150 each. But as a grower/nursery owner, you can purchase Japanese maple seedlings for around a dollar each, and re-pot and sell them for a substantial profit.

The maple seedlings should be potted in #2 pots, with good potting soil and a tablespoon of slow release fertilizer blended in. If you order your seedlings early enough in the spring, and get them potted right away, you could have trees to sell in a few months, after the trees have leafed out and the root system has grown. By potting in #2 pots instead of #1s, any trees not sold the first year can simply be left in the larger pot to grow in size and value.

When the tree has grown to 3' high, transplant it into a #5 pot, which will allow it to grow even larger in size and value. Many growers skip this step and transplant their best small trees in #15 pots, which is the size preferred by landscapers for "specimen" trees. Don't worry if you have leftover Japanese maples at the end of the season. They are always in demand, and you'll be able to charge more next year, as the trees continue to grow.

Because retail customers have a hard time visualizing what the tree will look like at maturity, many growers set aside one or two of each species to be used as display trees around the nursery. They can be planted in the ground or planted in a large attractive wooden container to allow for easy moving. One grower sells several of these mature trees each year to customers who need an instant "focal point" for a new landscape, and who are willing to pay the $200 - $400 he charges for each tree.

CHAPTER 6

Value-Added Landscaping Plants

There are many unique "niche" markets that are often neglected by the mass retailers that offer excellent profit potential for growers. Most require only a bit of extra time, rather than expense. Here are a few ideas to get you started.

Table-Top Christmas Trees

With more and more people living in condos and apartments, there is an increasing demand for miniature Christmas trees. Two varieties, Italian stone pine (Pinus pinea) and Elwood cedar (Chamaecyparis lawsonia "Elwoodii") are widely used. In colder parts of the country, Michigan State University researchers have picked Serbian spruce (Picea omorika), White Spruce (Picea glauca var. densata), Colorado spruce (Picea pungens) and Noble fir (Albies procera) as the best for a table-top tree.

Bonsai

From tiny trees barely six inches high to mature maples just eighteen inches high, the world of bonsai contains many surprises. Bonsai is the Japanese technique of stunting trees and shrubs without altering the natural appearance. Most bonsai trees are developed from regular nursery stock while still young enough to train. Some of the most popular are:

Evergreens – Atlas Cedar, Hinoki Cypress, Dwarf Norway Spruce, Dwarf White Spruce, Yeddo Spruce, Japanese White Pine, Sargent Juniper, Bar Harbor Juniper, Prostrate Juniper, Dwarf Japanese Yew.

Deciduous – Trident Maple, Japanese Maple, Japanese Hornbeam, Chinese Hackberry, Ginkgo, Deciduous Japanese Holly, Pieris japonica, Wisteria Floribunda, Sargent Crabapple, Scarlet Firethorn (Pyracantha) and Paper Birch.

Bonsai plants are sold in three types, starter plants, trained plants and specimen plants. Starter plants are small seedlings in 3-4" pots that are sold individually or in small assortments of six or so to bonsai enthusiasts who want to train their own plants. Prices vary according to age, shape of the plant and scarcity.

Trained bonsai are plants that have been "trained" to their first ceramic pot. They are in wide demand, as the buyer can see what the plant will look like as a bonsai subject, yet it will be young and small enough to be affordable. Prices range from $10 to $60, depending on size and beauty. Also popular in this price range are "mini-gardens" of two to five plants artistically arranged in one bowl.

Specimen bonsai plants. As your starts mature and you train them, set aside a few choice plants to mature for future sale as specimen plants. Prices are determined mostly by artistic appeal at this stage, but many prime specimens fetch hundreds of dollars.

Trellised Plants

Training a vining plant, such as a clemantis, on a simple trellis, rather than just on a stake is an excellent way to add value to the price of a plant – often double! Cedar fencing boards, sold at most lumberyards, can be ripped into narrow strips and assembled into a trellis, using a basic electric stapler or brad nailer. The larger pot sizes, such as #3 & #5 are best for this, as they provide more stability to prevent the top-heavy plants from tipping over.

Turning Shrubs into Trees

Many shrubs are quite lovely as trees, and because they are not as widely available as the basic shrubs, can bring a premium of 50-100% for just a small amount of work. The training is simple – just prune all the side branches, leaving only the branch called the "central leader". Stake the central leader, and let it grow until it reaches the height you want, pinching off side shoots. Then cut the top of the central leader to encourage a bushy head.

Each shrub species has a different growth habit, so you'll have to experiment as you go. Here are a few shrubs that are often used for tree training: Azalea, Callistemon, Camellia, Cotinus, Escallonia, Fuschia, Gardenia, Hibiscus, Ilex, Lantana, Laurus, Ligustrum, Photinia and Pyracantha.

Hpertufa Plant Containers

How can you sell a $3 plant for $20? It's easy to do, if you make a simple plant container using hypertufa. Hypertufa is an artificial stone that's easy to make, using Portland cement, sand peat and perlite.

For many years, alpine garden enthusiasts used a natural volcanic rock called tufa to make plant containers. Tufa is a lightweight, porous rock that is easy to shape. Because the aggregate used in hypertufa (perlite) is also lightweight, the plant containers made from hypertufa are also porous, light and freezeproof.

The basic formula for hypertufa is simple: 3 parts Portland cement, 4 parts peat, and five parts perlite. Just like any recipe, there are many variations of this basic formula. Plant containers can be large or small, free-form or traditional in shape. Succulents and ground covers are popular plant material for hypertufa plant containers.

There are several educational videos (www.youtube.com) that will show you how to make hypertufa plant containers. Just do a search at Youtube.com for "hypertufa". A web search for hypertufa will also lead you to several other tutorials as well.

Selling Your Landscaping Plants

Most small nurseries will do far better selling their plants directly to the retail public and landscapers. You'll get top dollar for your plants, and, unlike selling wholesale, you'll get paid when the customer buys the plant. Local regulations may determine how you sell your plants. Because of zoning regulations, for example, you may be restricted to rural locations or certain sizes. Check with local authorities to find out what is permitted in your location.

Because landscaping plant sales are seasonal, only advertise during your prime selling season, when the bulk of your sales will be made. For most growers, that's from early spring to fall. The free advertising-only papers, with names like "Little Nickel" and "Penny Saver" are a great place to run ads for your plants, listing what you have (trees, shrubs and groundcovers, for example) and a phone number and hours. You can also run free ads online at www.craigslist.com

You can also post flyers and cards at stores and other bulletin board locations. A local grower whose specialty is bamboo uses only 3x5 cards on bulletin boards for advertising, yet has a thriving business.

What if your local regulations don't permit regular retail sales? Try a garage sale or tag sale, which is allowed in almost all areas.

Be specific in your garage sale ad so everyone reading the ad will know you're selling just plants. Here's an example: Surplus Landscape Plants. 423 Plants must be sold this weekend! Saturday only, June 16th 9 a.m. to 3 p.m. 123 Elm Street – Mt. Vernon. Hundreds of plants – Most $8 each. Japanese maples, spirea, privet, juniper, escallonia and many more.

One grower reports selling $2,000 to $3,000 worth of plants in a weekend using simple ads like this in his local newspaper. Another approach is to have a weekend sale as a fundraiser for your local charity, church group or nonprofit, with a percentage (30-50% is typical) going to the organization.

Another profitable approach that allows you to get most of the retail price is to sell to landscapers. They expect a 20-25% discount off retail prices, and buy plants year-round, both for new landscaping jobs and replacement plants. Think about developing a mailing list of all the local landscapers, then mailing a flyer to them on a regular basis, with plant listings, sales, and plant ideas.

Farmer's Markets & Flea Markets

Both these markets can be a great way to retail your plants. You'll pay a small fee for the space, but in return can expect a good volume of walk-by customers. You'll also find these markets are an excellent place to make contact with future customers, so pass out flyers and cards to all who stop by.

Pre-Selling Your Plants

If you plan to wholesale plants, you'll need to begin selling long before the plants will be ready for sale. Visit retail nurseries, landscapers and stores, and tell them about your plans, what plants you will have available, sizes and quantities. Ask them for suggestions and advice. You must remember that in addition to growing what the customers want, you need to let them know you have it, and persuade them to buy from you. Invite them to your nursery to see what you're doing.

CHAPTER 7

Ornamental Grasses

The grass family, Graminaeae, are the most important plant family on earth, since they include the cereal grains such as barley, corn, oats, rice and wheat. Without grasses, life as we know it today would not exist.

There are over 10,000 known species of grasses, but only a few hundred of those are called "ornamental grasses" because of their exceptional color or form. Many of these have been popular for hundreds of years in Europe and Asia.

In North America, the ornamental grasses are enjoying a surge of popularity. They range in size from low-growing six-inch tufts to twenty-foot giants. Landscape designers love them because they can be used in so many ways – ground covers, specimen plants, in borders or near ponds and streams, as privacy screens and in rock gardens.

Several cities are using ornamental grasses for urban landscaping because they are so tolerant of air pollution and poor soil. In addition, the ornamental grasses are also being used more and more by decorators and floral designers as cut flowers and everlastings (dried flowers).

Thanks to this growing popularity, many nurseries are struggling to keep up with the demand. Ornamental grasses are ideal for the beginning grower, as few insects or diseases bother them, and you can sell your first crop in just one season.

Best Ornamental Grasses for Landscaping

Of the hundreds of ornamental grasses, these twenty are among the most popular with landscapers and retail plant buyers. Keep in mind that there are large regional variations. For example, a grass that is popular in milder climates will not survive in colder regions.

In addition, plants become "hot" then cool in popularity when too many landscapes feature the same plants. As you read the catalogs and web sites of the wholesale growers listed in the resource section, you'll notice that plant breeders are producing dozens of variations within a species, so the choices continue to multiply year by year.

Pay particular attention to the hardiness information listed for the plants. If a plant is listed as being hardy in zone 6, for example, that means it will likely survive the winter in that zone, but not in colder zones. You can find your zone in the U.S. Department of Agriculture's "Hardiness Zone Map" online at: www.garden.org/zipzone or check with your local agricultural extension office.

BLUE FESCUE – Festuce ovina glauca. This short plant produces silver blue clumps of foliage about six to twelve inches tall. Because the foliage lasts year-round, it's popular for ground covers and rock gardens. It's hardy to zone 4 and prefers cooler weather. It will not do well in clay soils and requires good drainage to thrive.

BLUE LYME GRASS – Elymus arenariius. Sometimes called wild rye, this is the bluest of the blue ornamental grasses. It's tough, and spreads quickly by underground rhizomes. Because of these traits, it's used widely for erosion control. When mature, the plants are about thirty inches tall. Hardy to zone 4.

BLUE OAT GRASS – Helictotrichon sempervirens. When mature, this ornamental grass looks like a blue hedgehog. It's hardy to zone 4, with lovely blooms in May. Blue oat grass prefers a well-drained soil and plenty of sun.

BULBOUS OAT GRASS – Arrhenatherum elatius bulbosum "variegatum". This attractive ornamental grass forms one -foot tall clumps of white and green striped leaves. It's hardy to zone 4, prefers a moist cool climate, and tolerates poor soil well

CRIMSON FOUNTAIN GRASS – Pennisetum setaceum. One of the most popular fountain grasses, because of its beautiful reddish-purple flowers. The plant will grow to four feet, with flower spikes a foot long. Hardy to zone 4, it prefers full sun.

EULALIA GRASS – Miscanthus sinensis. This species has been grown in Asia for centuries and became popular in North America during the Victorian era. It's a large plant, reaching seven feet in height under ideal growing conditions, so be sure to give it lots of growing room. It's hardy to zone 4 and prefers full sun.

FEATHERED REED GRASS – Calamagrostis acutiflora stricta. Feather reed grass is one of the best ornamental grasses. It's easy to grow, tolerates most soils and drought, and is hardy to zone 5. The purple flowers change from purple to buff, and last into the winter.

FOUNTAIN GRASS – Pennisetum alopecuroides. Fountain grass is one of the most popular ornamental grasses with gardeners today. It produces mounds of six-inch long flower heads, which bloom through October. Hardy to zone 5, it grows up to five feet tall.

GIANT MISCANTHUS – Miscanthus floridulus. This easy-to-grow warm-season grass is a striking specimen plant that reaches ten feet in height. It's hardy to zone 6 and prefers well- drained soil. It will tolerate shade or full sun.

GIANT REED – Arundo donax. This giant of a grass can grow to twenty feet in height, with bamboo- like stalks. With less than ideal conditions, it will top out at twelve feet. It's hardy to zone 6.

MAIDEN GRASS – Miscanthus sinesis "Gracillimus". With its slender blades reaching seven feet in length, this is one of the most formal of the larger grasses. The plant flowers in October and is hardy to zone 4. The leaves turn color in the fall after a few frosts, looking like dried corn husks, but stay attractive through the winter.

NORTHERN SEA OATS – Chasmanthium latifolium. Sea oats look like a three-foot tall bamboo plant at first glance. It's hardy through zone 4, and prefers shade and a moist, rich soil. The leaves turn a bright bronze color in the fall. The plant is widely used as a taller ground cover, and as a dried plant for flower arrangements.

PLUME GRASS – Erianthus ravennae. This plant is also called Ravenna grass or northern pampas grass because it is quite similar to pampas grass, but much hardier, thriving in zone 5. It will reach a height of fifteen feet in zone 7, and 8-10 feet in zone 5. Plume grass prefers fertile soil, full sun and a well-drained growing area.

PURPLE MOOR GRASS – Molinia caerulea. Purple moor grass comes in many forms. Because the slightest breeze sets the stems in motion, it's sometimes called dancing grass. The tall form of purple moor grass, "Windspiel", grows to six feet tall, with purple flowers in mid-summer. The small form, "Variegata", reaches three feet in height. Both are hardy to zone 5 and prefer moist soil and full sun.

RIBBON GRASS – Phalaris arundinacea "Picta". This old gardener's favorite is sometimes nicknamed "gardener's garters" and is quite invasive, spreading via underground rhizomes like bamboo. It grows quickly to three feet, forming bright green foliage with creamy stripes. It's hardy in zone 4 and tolerates a wide range of soil and moisture conditions.

SILVER FEATHER GRASS – Miscanthus sinensis "Silberfeder". This variation of the miscanthus species was introduced in 1967 by Dr. Hans Simon. The white fan shaped blooms are a bit more graceful than maiden grass, and bloom in August, a month earlier than most. This is a big advantage in colder climates, where a late bloomer might get caught in an early frost. It's hardy to zone 5.

SWITCH GRASS – Panicum virgatum. Switch grass is a native of the North American prairies that has been used by the Soil Conservation Service for many years for erosion control and wildlife cover. It grows four to six feet tall, with roots extending twice as deep. It's hardy to zone 3, and tolerates a wide variety of soils and growing conditions.

TUFTED HAIR GRASS – Deschampsia caespitosa. This cool season plant forms deep green tufts that grow up to two feet tall. It will thrive in a moist spot that has partial shade. The delicate flowers appear in June, and last well into the fall. There are several named cultivars available from nurseries that have especially showy flowers. The plant is evergreen, and hardy to zone 4.

VARIEGATED CORD GRASS – Spartina ebulosi "Aureo-marginata". This yellow striped plant is native to North America, reaching six feet in height. It's a tough plant, putting up with hot dry summers, extreme cold (hardy to zone 3) and poor soils. The plant turns bright yellow in the fall, and the flowers are popular for dried arrangements.

ZEBRA GRASS – Miscanthus sinensis "Zebrinus". Both Zebra grass, and a new cultivar, Porcupine grass "strictus", have bright green six-foot blades with yellow bands. Both prefer full sun and are hardy to zone 6. The zebra grass tends to droop at maturity, while the aptly named Porcupine grass is bristly and upright, forming a stiff, well-shaped clump.

Growing Ornamental Grasses

Ornamental grasses are easy plants to grow, but you must still give each plant it's best chance to thrive by picking the right spot for it. Think about the plant's needs. Does it prefer sun or shade?

Clayey or sandy soil, elbow room or crowding? Be sure to select plants that are suited to your growing conditions.

To get your ornamental grass nursery off to a good start, you'll need to buy properly labeled plants from a nursery that specializes in ornamental grasses (see the resource section). Be sure the plant is hardy in your hardiness zone – many nurseries provide that information in their catalogs or web sites.

Most ornamental grasses do best in full sun. If you growing area does not have full sun, you can still grow many varieties with less sun than recommended. The plants will not get a big or bushy, but they will still grow. As a general rule, the wider the leaves of an ornamental grass, the greater the shade tolerance.

When starting with purchased plants, prepare the planting area or potting soil well before your plants arrive so there will be no delays in getting them in the ground. Most ornamental grasses do not need fertilizing. In fact, fertilizer could be harmful to the plants, causing soft growth and droopy plants.

Once ornamental grasses are established, they require little care. In dry climates, you'll need to irrigate or water to keep the plants from drying out. Most grasses will require a yearly cutting back to look best. This should be done in late winter or early spring before new growth starts.

To provide more plants for sale, divide and transplant your ornamental grasses. The best time for cool season growers such as the fescues is in the fall. Warm season growers, such as miscanthus, should be divided and transplanted in the spring.

To divide a plant, dig up a clump, getting as many roots as possible. Some plants can be pulled apart by hand, while other require an axe or machete. Be sure that each divided clump has at least one stem and a few roots. Remember, the more divisions you make, the more plants you will have to sell.

When you re-plant the divided clumps, allow enough space for growth. A good rule of thumb is to space the plants half as far apart as they are tall at maturity. If you are planning to leave the plants in their new location permanently, space them as far apart as they are tall at maturity.

Another factor to remember when dividing and replanting is the size plants you plan to sell. Talk to prospective customers such as landscapers or garden centers to find out the sizes they want to buy. Many growers offer a variety of sizes, from field clumps to five-gallon container- grown plants. Ornamental grasses used mainly for groundcovers should be grown in flats of four-inch pots.

Dried Ornamental Grasses

Until just a few years ago, most dried grasses (also called "everlastings") sold in North America were imported. Now more and more are being grown in the U.S. and Canada, as consumer preferences shift from the brightly dyed imports to natural colors. Here, in alphabetical order by common name are the top ten annual (A) and perennial(P) ornamental grasses.

Canary Grass. (A) Phalaris canariensis

Cloud Grass. (A) Agrostis ebulosi

Eulalia Grass. (P) Miscanthus sinensis

Hare's Tail Grass (A) Lagurus ovatus

Love Grass (P) Eragristis trichodes

Northern Sea Oats (P) Chasmanthium latifolium

Plume Grass (P) Erianthus ravannae

Quaking Grass (A) Briza maxima or Briza minor

Rabbit Tail Grass (A) Polypogon monspeliensis

Switch Grass (P) Panicum virgatum

Growing Ornamental Grasses for Drying

Annual grasses are as easy to grow as marigolds. Sow the seeds outdoors after all danger of frost is past. For an earlier bloom, plant indoors or in a greenhouse, and transplant the seedlings later. With good sun and fertile, well-drained soil, you'll have flowers by mid-August.

Perennial grasses are normally bought as plants rather than seeds. Use the rule of thumb given earlier for spacing when you plant your clumps. For most plants, spring planting will give you the best survival rate, and more vigorous growth.

Harvesting Ornamental Grasses for Drying

It is extremely important to pick the flowers just as they are expanding from the leaves of the plant. Even though this might seem too early, it is really the best time. Why? If you wait until the flower is mature, it will shatter as it dries. The longer you wait, the greater the chances of shattering.

Drying Ornamental Grasses

All the everlasting grasses just listed are "natural" everlastings, meaning they can be air dries – a simple and quick method. You'll need an enclosed area that's dry, shady or dark to prevent the colors from fading, and good air circulation. A screened porch, barn loft, shed or basement will do. An inexpensive box fan will provide air circulation if there is no natural air movement. Spaced wires or clotheslines in the drying area provide hanging space for the everlastings.

If you wrap the bunches at the stem ends with rubber bands, they will hold the stems tightly as the stems dry and shrink. To hang the bunches, use a simple "S" hook (a paper clip is just the right size) with one end hooked under the rubber band and the other end over the hanging wire.

To dry everlastings upright, chicken or rabbit fencing, with a 1" hex mesh, stapled to a wood frame, provides a good support platform. It works well for those delicate flowers that could be crushed together in a bunch. You can stack up the drying frames to provide even more drying area.

Dyeing Ornamental Grasses

Dyeing your harvest can add to the appeal, and result in more sales, especially to florists and craft shops. Here's a simple, easy-to-use method for dyeing:

For each quart of water, use 1/2 tsp. aniline dye or 2-4 oz. clothing dye, and 8 tsp. alum or 1 tsp. acetic acid. Dissolve the alum or acetic acid in water, bring to a boil, then add the dye.

Dip bunches of dried flowers, holding the heads down, in the hot dye solution. Keep them in the solution until the color is the shade you want, then gently tap to remove excess moisture and hang to dry.

Markets for both natural and dyed ornamental grasses include farmer's markets, florists, gift shops, craft shops and value-added products such as wreaths and floral arrangement.

CHAPTER 8

Profitable Flowers

Flowers are a perfect cash crop, because they are easy to grow, produce quickly and supply an income throughout the season. In addition, the startup costs can be low because you only need to buy seeds and supply labor.

If you're like most beginning growers, you'll want to start small to get a feel for what works best in your area, both for growing and marketing. Since each region has several unique micro-climates, you'll discover that some flowers will do great in your garden and some poorly.

The same goes for markets. One grower may sell their entire flower crop at the Farmer's Market, while another will do best selling dried flowers (everlastings) to craft shops and florists. You can't learn this overnight, so take my advice and "tip-toe" into this new world of growing flowers for sale. That way, you'll learn without making too many costly mistakes.

START YOUR OWN BACKYARD PLANT NURSERY

Best Flowers to Grow

I surveyed flower growers around the country and asked them to name the flowers that were:

- Easiest to grow.
- Most reliable.
- Most productive.
- Most in demand.

Start with these proven favorites your first growing season, then experiment with other varieties, adding new flowers to your growing list each year for trials. In time you'll know what grows best in your micro-climate and which flowers are most in demand from your customers.

Both the botanical name and the common name are listed for the flowers. You'll find most flowers listed by botanical name in seed and nursery catalogs, but your retail customers will usually use the common name.

Best annual flowers to grow

Ageratum (Floss flower)

- Tall growing "Blue Horizon" and "Florist's White" are two cultivars ideal for market growers.
- Start indoors or in greenhouse six to eight weeks before last frost date, then plant in rows 12" apart.
- Harvest when the flowers begin to open.

Antirrhinum (Snap Dragon)

- The long-stemmed "Rocket" cultivar popular with growers.

- Harvest when the flowers are half open.

- Start indoors eight weeks before last frost date, the plant in garden 12" apart.

- Support netting will help the flowers avoid wind damage.

- Harvest when half the flowers are open.

Celosia

- Christata, Plumosa and Spicata are best varieties for cutting.

- Can be started indoors, or direct seeded in the garden after last frost.

- This is a large plant, so allow 12" to 18" between plants.

- Harvest "Cristata" when flowers are fully open, the others when the flowers are almost fully open.

Consolida Ambigua (Larkspur)

- Widely used by florists and a very productive plant in the garden.

- Needs six weeks of cold exposure (below 55 degrees F)

- Can be direct seeded in garden.

- Harvest when one-third of the flowers are open and put stems in water to increase vase life.

Cosmos

- Short-lived after harvest, so best for local sales, such as Farmer's markets.

- Best started indoors, as they are day length sensitive.
- Popular cultivars include "Sensation", "Imperial" and "Versailles."
- Harvest when the petals begin to open.
- Cut long stems to encourage branching (and more stems) below your cut.

Euphorbia Marginata (Snow on the Mountain)

- Direct seed in garden after last frost day of spring.
- Harvest when upper leaves are all white and lower leaves are white-lined.
- Dipping the stems in hot water for ten minutes will stop sap bleeding.

Godetia (Satin Flower)

- Prefers temperatures under 75 degrees.
- Space plants two feet apart for a spray of blooms.
- Vase life up to two weeks.
- Harvest when the first flower on stem is completely open.

Gomphrena (Globe Amaranth)

- Start seeds indoors, then transplant to the garden after the last frost
- Space plants 9" to 12" apart in the row.
- Harvest when most flowers have full color.
- Also popular as a dried flower.

Helianthus Annuus (Sunflower)

- Enjoying a surge in popularity.
- Best cutting sunflowers are the new pollenAless cultivars, such as "Sunbeam".
- Can be direct seeded 9" to 12" apart in the garden, or transplanted.
- Harvest when the petals are fully open, and put in water.

Rudbeckia (Black-eyed Susan)

- Rudbeckia hirta "Indian Summer" most popular annual with commercial growers.
- Vase life of ten days.
- Harvest before petals are fully open, and place in a bucket of water with preservative to finish opening.

Salvia

- Popular species include S. horminum, S. farinacea and S. coccinea.
- Plants need plenty of elbow room, so allow two feet between plants.
- Harvest after one or two florets have opened.

Zinnia

- Loves hot, dry weather.
- Top grower picks: "Giant Dalhia Bluepoint", "State Fair" and "Oklahoma".

- Direct seed in the garden every two weeks for continuous cutting.
- Harvest when the flowers are fully open.
- Vase life of five to seven days.

Best Perennial Flowers to Grow

Achillea (Yarrow)

- Grower favorites include A. filipendula, A. millefolium and A. ptarmica.
- Can be grown from seed or plant starts.
- A fast multiplier, it can produce hundreds of new plants in two or three years.
- Harvest when pollen appears on fully opened flowers. Vase life of up to twelve days (A.ptarmica only lasts five to seven days).
- A good choice for air drying also.

Allium

- Plant bulbs in garden two to three inches apart, where they will rapidly multiply.
- Grower favorites include: A. aflatunense, A. giganteum and A. sphaerocephalon.
- Vase life of up to fourteen days.
- Harvest when a third of the florets are open.

Asclepias (Butterfly Weed)

- Grower favorites include A. tuberose, A. incarnate and A. Curassavica.
- Vase life up to two weeks.
- Put stems in 120-degree water for a minute after cutting to stop sap bleeding.

Aster

- The September aster (Aster ericoides), New England aster (Aster novaeA angliae) and the New York aster (Aster noviAbelgii) are the best species for cut flower growers.
- Space one to two feet apart in the garden.
- Harvest when two or three flowers are open.
- Vase life of five to seven days.

Astilbe (False Goat's Beard)

- Start with plants rather than seeds.
- Harvest when two florets are open.
- Vase life of up to twelve days.
- To harvest for drying, wait until flowers are completely open.

Buddleia Davidii (Butterfly Bush)

- Harvest when half the flowers are open.
- Vase life of five to eight days.
- Buy a "Mother" plant, then start more from rooted cuttings.

Chrysanthemum Leucanthemum (Shasta Daisy)

- Best started from seed.
- Space one foot apart in garden.
- Harvest when petals are half open.
- Vase life of seven to ten days.

Gypsophilia Paniculata (Perennial Baby's Breath)

- The sprays of small flowers make an excellent filler in floral arrangements. Florists use so much it's jokingly called the "florist's hamburger helper".
- Direct seed in the garden, spacing the plants two feet apart. Harvest when most of the flowers are open.
- Also a popular flower for drying.

Lavandula (Lavender)

- This Mediterranean native prefers a dry, sunny climate and well-drained soil.
- Harvest when the flowers begin to open.
- Vase life of eight to ten days.
- Another good choice for drying.

Veronica Longifolia (Speedwell)

- Start seed indoors, then transplant to garden, spacing plants one foot apart.
- Harvest when half the tiny flowers are open.
- Place in preservative-treated water after cutting for longest vase life.

Growing Cut Flowers

Most flowers prefer a well-drained soil, with a neutral pH, and lots of organic matter. If you're fortunate enough to have a growing area with perfect soil, consider yourself lucky. If not, you can create a growing environment for flowers, using compost, cover crops and soil amendments.

Creating Raised Beds

Creating raised beds in your garden can "jump-start" your flower growing business, by providing the good drainage so necessary for healthy flowers (flowers dislike wet feet!). In addition to being easy to work, raised beds can also produce greater yields. Most flower growers use a tiller or small tractor to create raised beds. Troy-Built, for example, makes a "hiller" attachment for their larger tillers that creates a raised bed.

Wind Protection

Your flower growing beds will need wind protection to prevent stem and bloom damage. If your garden site doesn't have buildings, shrubs or trees now to provide a windbreak, plant a row of shrubs you can cut (see "woody ornamentals" chapter for ideas).

According to the U.S.D.A., a windbreak is effective for about eight times its height. Planting a windbreak of eight foot tall shrubs every sixty feet or so will help prevent wind damage to your flowers as well as providing woody ornamental material to harvest and sell

Drip Irrigation

Flowers need water to grow, so you'll need to provide irrigation water to all the raised flower beds in your garden. Growers usually figure an inch of water per week during the growing season. If you have a small flower garden, watering with a hose may be the best method until you expand the growing area.

Water in the early evening after it's started to cool down provides water for night growth and minimizes evaporation losses. Some flowers, such as roses, snapdragons and zinnias, should be watered only at the base to avoid disease problems.

For most growers, setting up a simple drip irrigation system will save time and money, because drip irrigation gets the water right to the base of the plant so you're not wasting water. In addition, drip irrigation reduces water loss from evaporation. You'll likely find the modest cost of a drip system pays for itself the first growing season in reduced water usage.

Contact Dripworks for free, expert advice in setting up a system for your flower garden. A drip tape system can handle up to several acres. The drip tape is easy to move around, so you can re-arrange the system as your garden changes each year. You can also visit their web site, www.dripworks.com to learn more about drip irrigation, as well as view their online catalog.

Soil Preparation

If you're growing for market, you want an abundance of beautiful, healthy flowers to sell. The only way to accomplish that is to spend the time to prepare your garden soil to produce those fabulous flowers! There's an old saying among organic gardeners: "Feed your soil, not your plants", and it's even more true for market growers, whose crops bring the highest prices when they are at the peak of perfection.

The two "secret" ingredients for healthy soil (and plants) are compost and cover crops. Both build soil fertility and add organic matter to the soil. At this point, you may be wondering, "Why not just add a sack or two of 15-30-15 fertilizer and be done with it?" Because using organic methods that build the soil will produce healthy plants that are more pest-resistant. So you'll be able to avoid using pesticides and herbicides that are harmful to you, your family, your neighbors and ultimately, the world around you.

For the same reasons you should only use organic fertilizers to grow your flowers – here's why. Chemical fertilizers tend to stimulate rapid growth but weaken the plants and make them prone to disease and insect damage. Organic fertilizers produce a steady, less stressed growth rate, which results in healthier plants with strong stems and bigger, brighter blooms.

I don't have the space here to climb on my organic soapbox to give you a long lecture, but, trust me, you'll be better off, and your flowers will thrive if you go organic. Most organic growers also find, as a "fringe benefit", that their flowers sell better when they're labeled "Organically Grown".

Soil Testing

It's a good idea to test the soil where you plan to start your flower garden. In most areas, your local County Extension office can either send your soil samples to a laboratory for testing or give you a list of capable testing labs. The cost is modest, and you'll get a nutrient analysis that will help you to build up the deficient areas.

Compost

Most growers will need more compost than they can produce on-site, unless there are lots of farm animals to help out. Compost will help loosen up clay soils, aid water retention in sandy soils, and help your flowers grow big, strong and beautiful. If you're not composting now, start!

A quick trip to the library will get you started with the best methods and materials. Even if you can't produce enough compost for all your flowerbeds, it will allow you to recycle materials that would otherwise be wasted, such as stalks, grass clippings and prunings from your garden.

For large quantities of compost, you'll need to find a commercial composter. Many municipalities now sell compost at reasonable prices, and you can pick it up if you have a truck or trailer or arrange to have it delivered. You can also check with your local organic certification agency for a list of certified organic composters in your area, and purchase from one of them.

Cover Crops

Cover crops are widely used by organic growers to build soil fertility, protect against erosion and add organic matter to the soil. Many cover crops, such as the clovers, add nitrogen to the soil as they grow. You can either plant a cover crop in the fall, after you've harvested your annual flowers, or use a cover crop in "rotation" with your flowers. For example, you might plant flowers in a garden bed one year, then plant a cover crop in that same bed the next year to build soil fertility.

Popular spring-seeded cover crops include:

- BlackAeyed peas.
- Buckwheat.
- Cowpeas.
- Soybeans.

Fall-seeded cover crops include:

- Austrian winter peas.
- Clovers – crimson and sweet clover.
- Fava beans.
- Oats.
- Vetch – common, hairy vetch and purple vetch.

Starting Plants

If you're like most growers, you'll end up with a mix of annuals, perennials and bulbs. You can start most of them yourself, either by direct-seeding in the garden or indoors or in a greenhouse. Some – mostly perennials and bulbs – should be purchased the first time. Once they are established, you'll be able to divide the plants to increase your stock, instead of buying more. One of the first steps in starting your flower business is to get a business license or state sales tax number. Then, you'll have proof that you're a "real" business and qualified for wholesale prices from nurseries and other suppliers.

Starting out, you'll want to buy a "flat" of each perennial flower you plan to grow in your flower garden. This is a very inexpensive way to start out, as you'll be paying wholesale prices (As low as 20%-30% of retail), and you'll be able to propagate your perennials in a year or two for free plants.

Try to purchase your plants as close to home as possible, to minimize shipping damage and plant stress. In most areas, you'll be able to find an in-state nursery that has just the variety you're looking for. Ideally, they will be close enough for you to pick up your plants and a few growing tips as well. Check with the nursery association for your state – that's a good place to start your search for a nursery that specializes in the plants you're looking for. To find it, do an internet search for "your state nursery association."

Flower Production Tips

Making the shift from a "hobby" to a commercial flower grower requires you to take a fresh look at every phase of your growing process to make sure that you're working efficiently. Fortunately, there are many low-tech affordable tools that can help you reduce the amount of time spent on the routine tasks, such as seeding, weeding and watering. As mentioned earlier, drip irrigation allows you to simply turn on the tap, rather than hand watering for hours. Here are some other labor-saving tools most growers find essential for profitable flower growing.

Mulching

For a smaller garden, loose mulches such as shredded bark and straw can be an effective weed control. Most market flower growers use a polypropylene weed barrier fabric, cutting square holes at the desired spacing for the flowers being grown. While it costs more than a black plastic mulch, it can be pulled up and re-used for several years, so the "life-cycle" cost is quite low. It's a "one-way" barrier, so air and water can pass through, but weeds are blocked.

Mechanical Seeding

For flowers that can be direct seeded in the garden, such as zinnia, a simple push seeder can save hours (and your back!) It's important to keep the rows as straight as possible to make weeding easier, so run a string between a stake at each end of the row as a guide. The "Earthway" seeder, available from Johnny's Seeds, is my favorite, as it's inexpensive to buy and easy to operate.

Pest Control

Pest control is more important with flowers than other crops, as a flawless appearance is essential to getting top prices. Organic growers have a variety of tools in their pest control toolbag, including:

- **"Sticky traps"** – as the name implies, are covered with a sticky substance that traps insects. They are available in insect's two favorite colors, yellow and blue. Blue, for example, attracts thrips, a common flower pest.
- **Insecticidal soaps** – that dissolve the membranes of many insects.
- **Pyrethrums** – a compound derived from a chrysanthemum relative that can paralyze many insect pests.
- **Bt** – a bacteria that destroys an insect's digestive system.
- **Neem** – An extract of the Neem tree that repels insects.

Flower Netting

The long flower stems preferred by flower buyers are prone to wind damage, unless they are supported as they grow. In a small flower bed, a support, such as twine or temporary fencing, around the perimeter can help hold up the plant stems as they grow.

Most commercial flower growers use a polypropylene support netting with a 6" mesh to support flowers with longer stems. The netting is applied after you've planted, laid the drip irrigation tape, and mulched. The netting is stretched between stakes at the edges of the bed, with the height depending on the flower variety being grown in the bed.

Harvesting Flowers

Harvesting needs to be done at the proper stage for each flower variety. The correct time is listed for the more popular flowers earlier in this guide. Seed suppliers will also list the correct harvest time (petals first opening – fully open flowers, for example) for individual flowers.

"The Flower Farmer", listed in the resource section, has a comprehensive chapter on the best harvesting practices for almost a hundred individual flower varieties. In addition, there are instructions for building an inexpensive flower cooler, using an insulated box and an ordinary window air-conditioner. A cooler can keep your flowers fresher.

It's best to harvest early in the morning, when the flower's water content is highest. Wait until just after the dew has dried to avoid mildew problems. Flowers can be dry picked, and placed in water later, or placed in a bucket of water with preservative as you pick. Most seed suppliers, such as Johnny's Seeds, sell Floralife preservative in bulk. The preservative increases the life and quality of the cut flowers immensely.

Growing Flowers for Drying

Acroclinium (Helipterum roseum)

These everlasting flowers produce an abundance of flowers all through the growing season, and are available in white and shades of yellow, pink and red.

Acroclinium prefers a well-drained, slightly acid soil, with full sun and not too much wind. It's considered an easy flower to grow, reaching a height of 18 – 24 inches. It needs a temperature of 55 -60 degrees to germinate, so you can plant indoors and transplant the seedlings or direct sow in the garden. In the northern U.S., growers sow seeds outdoors in May for a harvest starting in August and continuing on until the first frost.

Whether you direct seed or transplant, space the plants 8-12 inches apart in rows. To harvest, cut the stems just as the flowers start to open. Harvest daily. If you wait too long, the yellow centers will turn black. Strip the leaves off the stems. Bunch – ten or twelve stems to the bunch – and hang in a dark dry area with good air circulation.

Artemesia (Sweet Annie)

The foliage is a widely used filler material to provide a backdrop for the more colorful flowers. The gray-green color is essential for making herb wreaths. Silver King has better flowers, but Silver Queen has the best foliage. Johnny's has varieties that mature faster, and a scentless variety.

Artemesia is an extremely hardy perennial which grows quickly, requiring full sun and well-drained soil. After your first plants are established, you can start new ones by pulling up and replanting the new shoots spreading from the mother plant. Space your plants one foot apart to encourage bushy growth. This spacing should yield about six spikes of flowers.

If you plan to use the spikes of flowers, harvest after the flowers have formed. If you plan to only use the foliage, harvest anytime. Hang the stems in small bunches to dry. If you plan to use your harvest for wreaths, wind it around the wire frame while it's still fresh, using wire to hold it in place.

Baby's Breath (Gypsophilia)

This flower is widely used as a filler in floral arrangements. "Bristol Fairy" and "Double Snowflake" are popular varieties because of the large number of double blooms. Be sure to plant the perennial varieties, because the annual (Gypsophilia elegans) turns a dull gray when dried.

Gypsophilia prefers a sunny spot with well-drained, well-limed soil. It is best to start with transplants from a nursery. Because it's a perennial, it will not produce flowers the first season. The second and following years, it will produce giant clouds of tiny blooms. To allow plenty of room for these clouds, space the plants about three feet apart.

Harvest Gypsophilia when most flowers are open. If you leave about a foot of stem, you can get a second cutting. After the second cutting, and before the first frost, cut the whole plant back to just above the ground. Hang the harvested clumps upside down to dry. The stems become brittle after drying but can be kept more flexible by soaking the stems in glycerine.

Celosia (Celosia cristata)

This hardy annual, sometimes called "Cockscomb" because of the unique texture of the blooms, produces large plumes of showy flowers in a variety of colors. The tall varieties sell best, although you should consider the dwarf varieties if you have a windy growing area.

Celosia prefers lots of sun, well-drained rich soil, and very little water. Start indoors about a month before the last frost date in your area. When the seedling are one inch tall, transplant into 3-inch pots and keep them indoors till all danger of frost is past. Then transplant to the garden, spacing the plants one to two feet apart. A wider spacing will produce more plumes.

Harvest the blooms all through the season. If you start picking early enough, you'll get new blooms on the side branches. Stand the stems upright in a wire screen (half-inch mesh galvanized hardware cloth) to dry. Keeping the drying area dark will help preserve the bright colors of the plumes.

Delphinium Larkspur (Delphinium ajacis)

Delphiniums are one of the most impressive flowers, with their stately form and colors ranging from blue to pure white to purple. The annual delphiniums are called larkspur. European commercial growers consider Delphinium ajacis to be the best species for dried flower production, because it's much easier and quicker to grow than the perennials.

Start your first plants from seed and keep them in a separate growing bed to control the spreading. Seeding every two weeks will stretch your harvest time. Larkspur gets tall, so wind protection is important. Stakes and netting work best, while some growers use compact varieties that do not require support.

Harvest the stems when the blossoms are half open. Strip the leaves and hang, head down, in a dark, well-ventilated drying area.

Feverfew (Chrysanthamum parthenium)

This old garden favorite is a heavy producer for the entire growing season. Unlike most of the other "mums", feverfew dries well. The small daisy-shaped flowers are an attractive addition to floral arrangements.

Feverfew is a hardy perennial that requires little care once established, and will self-seed each year. Space the plants one foot apart in the garden and provide plenty of sun. To get a second cutting, trim the plant back after the first harvest. Harvest the flowers as they bloom. To dry, strip the leaves from the stems and hang upside-down in small bunches.

Globe Amaranth (Gomphrena)

The globe amaranth looks a lot like a giant red clover blossom. It's a useful and popular flower for floral arrangements, and comes in pinks, purples and whites, reaching 18 inches in height at maturity.

Globe amaranth needs a warm, sunny location, as it's a tender annual. Make sure the soil is light and well-drained, as the plants do not like wet feet. Sow your seeds indoors in March, keeping the growing area at 75 degrees to insure germination. When the plants are about 4 inches tall, transplant them to 3-4-inch pots, and keep the temperature at 70 degrees. When daytime temperatures are above 70 degrees, transplant to the garden, spacing the plants 8 inches apart. As the plants are tall, support may be necessary.

Pick the blossoms just before full bloom, cutting the stems just above the branch. If you wait too long to pick, the blossoms are too brittle, and shatter after drying. Strip the leaves, and hang to dry, or dry heads-up using a wire screen for support. The plants will dry better with good air circulation.

Immortelle (Xeranthum annuum)

This hardy annual is a close relative of the strawflower, with colorful blooms and strong short stems. White is the best-selling color, with lavender second. It's as easy to grow as strawflowers and produces continuous blossoms through the growing season.

In milder climates, you can direct seed in the garden after the ground has warmed up. Some growers prefer to start their plants in flats, transplanting after the last frost date, and spacing them a foot apart in the garden.

Unlike many everlastings, immortelle flowers do not open further after harvest, so be sure to pick only after the flowers are fully open. Cut the stems, bunch, and hang upside down to dry.

Lavender (Lavendula)

Lavender is better known as a herb than as an everlasting, but the distinctive smell and small blossoms make it an ideal addition to wreaths and small bouquets. The leaves contain the same fragrant oil as the flowers, and can be used for sachets, teas and potpourri.

This hardy perennial, native to the Mediterranean, thrives on full sun and poor, sandy soil. Once your plants are established, you'll find lavender needs little attention. Buy plants to start your collection, then propagate more from cuttings. Pinch off the flower buds the first year to stimulate bushy growth.

To harvest, pick the stems as the flower buds begin to open. Strip the leaves off before hanging and save them for sachets or potpourri. Hang small bunches upside-down in a shady, well-ventilated area.

Love-In-A-Mist (Nigella damascene)

Nigella are old-fashioned annuals originating in the Mediterranean region. The common name comes from the appearance of the small blue or white flowers surrounded by the bright green filmy foliage, followed by the distinctive egg-shaped pods. Growers who sell everlastings at Farmer's Markets say nigella is one of the first to sell out.

Nigella is easy to grow, requiring only average soil and growing conditions. Sow the seeds directly in the spring, as soon as the weather allows. To extend the harvest, seed additional areas every two weeks through the spring. Space the plants 6A9 inches apart.

Colors available include white, purple, rose, pink, blue and lavender. The fresh green pods are often used in fresh flower designs, but the dried pods are more widely used. Europeans use nigella as a fresh cut flower. At maturity, when the seed pods are firm, bunch, and hang head down to dry in a shaded, well -ventilated area. Save the seeds for next year's crop.

Money Plant (Lunaria annua)

This old-fashioned plant was a favorite in grandmother's day, and it's still quite popular. It's a biennial, so you can expect a crop the second year after planting. The flowers can be used in fresh flower arrangements, but the main attraction is the "silver dollars" revealed when the seed pod cover is peeled off.

Lunaria prefers well-drained soil and even partial shade. Don't fertilize it, as that encourages foliage growth at the expense of seedpods. To get a crop the first year, start the seeds indoors in early spring. The seeds will germinate in a week or so at 65 degrees. Transplant the seedlings to your garden about the same time you would transplant tomatoes. Keep them spaced about a foot apart to encourage good air circulation. This should give you a crop of silver dollar pods the first season.

The alternative growing method is to seed directly in the garden in early summer and thinning to a one-foot spacing. The plants will over-winter, and you'll be harvesting pods early the next summer. To harvest, cut the stems when the seed pods are starting to turn from green to tan in color. Tie the stems in small bunches, and hang upside down to dry in a cool, dry place with good air circulation. About three weeks after harvesting, remove the brown outer husk by rubbing between your thumb and forefinger to reveal the silver disc inside. You'll normally get four or five stems per plant.

Statice (Limonium sinuatum)

This popular everlasting is a staple of florists, who use it as a filler in many traditional arrangements. It's easy to grow and dry, with tiny flowers of white, yellow, rose, blue and purple. The blues and purples produce the most blossoms, the yellows the least. Another popular variety is "Pink Poker" statice with its distinctive curved spikes of blooms.

In areas with mild winters, statice can be treated as a perennial. Most growers treat it as an annual, starting seedlings indoors, and transplanting outdoors when all danger of frost is past. Statice needs full sun and a neutral to alkaline soil. Space your transplants 12-18 inches apart.

Pick the stems when the blooms are three-quarters open and leave the foliage on the stems. Dry the stems by hanging upside down or standing the stems upright in a wire screen. The upright method prevents damage to the fragile fresh blossoms.

Strawflower (Helichrysum bracteatum)

Strawflowers are the ideal everlasting flower for the beginning grower, as they are easy to grow and produce an abundance of flowers with little effort. They also hold their color when dried better than most other everlastings. Dwarf varieties are only 12-18 inches tall, but the tall plants seem to produce the best mum-shaped flowers, and are easier to pick.

In most areas, you'll need to start seed indoors. The seeds will germinate in about two weeks at 65 degrees. Wait until the last frost before transplanting to the garden, spacing the plants about one foot apart.

You should pick the blossoms regularly during the harvest season. This encourages blossom production, and you'll get as many as three dozen blossoms per plant this way. Pick the blossoms just as the outer two or three rows of petals are opening. Tie the stems into bunches of ten or so, and hang upside-down in a shaded, well-ventilated area to dry.

Yarrow (Achillea filipendulina)

This tough perennial will survive heat, drought and neglect and still produce those lovely clusters of yellow flowers that are so popular. The golden yellow colors are the most desired for floral designs, with the medium clusters the most used size.

Start seeds indoors in the spring. Harden off the seedlings, and transplant to the garden in late spring or early summer. Your plants will flower the second year after planting. Once you have established yarrow plants, it's easy to simply divide the plants every three years. This keeps the plants healthier and provides you with an abundant supply of new plants.

Harvest the stems when the flowers are fully open, leaving the foliage on the stem. Hang the stem to dry in a dark, well-ventilated place.

Growing Everlastings

Dried flowers, also called everlastings because of their lifespan, are an ideal crop for the small grower. As a group, they're a forgiving bunch, easy to grow and easy to dry. Best of all, once you've dried your crop, there's no hurry to sell to avoid spoilage as with fresh cut flowers. Your dried flowers will keep just fine with reasonable care until sold, giving you the opportunity to maximize your profits by selling when you choose.

Most of the everlastings originated in dry climates, and do not like having their roots too wet. So you should pick a growing area that's naturally well-drained, or use raised beds with a growing soil that's been modified to drain well. The growing information given earlier for cut flowers, covering wind protection, drip irrigation, soil preparation, composting, cover crops, starting plants and production tips all apply equally to everlasting flowers.

Harvesting Everlastings

Late morning is the best time to harvest most everlastings. The morning dew has had a chance to dry, but the afternoon sun hasn't caused the blossoms to droop. Each flower is different. Statice, for example, can be picked every few days, while strawflowers need to be picked every day.

Most everlastings should be picked just before full bloom, because the bloom continues to mature even after picking. The leaves should usually be stripped off the stem right after picking – this allows better air circulation around the blossoms as they dry and prevents molding and mildewing.

Drying Everlastings

All the everlastings just listed are "natural" everlastings, which means that they can be simply air dried to preserve them. Beyond air drying, there are many exotic techniques used today to preserve flowers that use dessicants, glycerine, even freeze-drying. Until you've got a growing season or two behind you, stick to the basic air-drying techniques.

You'll need an enclosed area that dry, shady or dark (a dark spot helps hold vivid colors) with good air circulation. A screened porch, barn, shed or even basement will work. An inexpensive box fan can provide air circulation if there is no natural air movement. Spaced wires or clothesline in the drying area provide hanging space for the upside-down flower bunches.

If you wrap the bunches at the stem end with rubber bands, they will hold the stems tight as the stems dry and shrink. To dry flowers upright, rabbit fencing or galvanized hardware cloth with a tight mesh under one inch can be stapled to a wood frame for a support platform. It works well for those delicate flowers that would be crushed in a bunch. You can stack or hang the frames in several layers to provide even more drying area in a small space.

Woody Ornamentals

Woody ornamentals are trees and shrubs that grow back after cutting and have a "woody" outer layer on the branches. In recent years, woodies have become popular with floral designers, who use them extensively for filling out bouquets – especially the large arrangements done for hotels and events. Some popular woodies are everyday plants, like forsythia and lilac. Others are a bit more uncommon, such as corkscrew willow. All are perennials, so once you've planted them, they require little work other than cutting the branches at harvest time.

Woodies also make great season-stretchers, with spring blooms, like forsythia, to start the season, and berries and branches, like holly, in the fall to end the season. Speaking of seasons, be sure to get the cultivars that are hardy in your area. You'll find that information in most nursery catalogs, or you can ask the floriculture specialist at your county extension office. Many small floral growers find woodies can serve double-duty, by planting them as a harvestable windbreak.

Although most flower growers consider woodies a valuable addition to their cut flower and dried flower crops, many are choosing to specialize in woody ornamentals. One Wisconsin grower, John Zehrer, started out planting curly willow just to see how it would do. It grew like a weed, so he planted more, and added red osier dogwood, lilacs, golden ninebark, and several others. He found his woodies were in demand from a growing list of wholesale buyers, grocery stores, retail florists and farmer's markets. Today, he's harvesting thirty-five acres of woodies, with a season that extends from February through November.

John suggests that beginning growers avoid two mistakes he made when starting out. First, buy rooted cuttings (known in the nursery trade as "liners") and grow them out to a height of 18 inches before planting them in their final location. This will get you in production quicker and easier. John planted many of his first woodies too close together, so when they matured, there was no room to maneuver around them. He says to give them room to spread out, spacing rows 10-15 feet apart, and four feet between the plants.

Best Woody Ornamentals

Beautyberry (Callicarpa Americana)

- Produces berries on stems in the fall.
- Harvest entire stem to encourage new growth in spring.
- Vase life up to fourteen days.

Bittersweet (Celastrus scandens)

- Clusters of orange berries a popular fall seller.
- Needs a sturdy trellis to support the vines.
- Harvest entire stem for vigorous spring growth.

Bluebeard (Caryopteris clandonesis)

- Late summer bloomer, with blue flowers and silvery leaves.
- Very drought-tolerant.

- Flowers repeatedly after each cutting, from late summer to first frost.
- Harvest at full bloom, put stems in hot water.

Butterfly Bush (Buddleia davidii)

- Like bamboo, this plant grows so big, so fast, you can almost hear it growing.
- Start with one plant, then root cuttings for many more.
- Cut stems six inches from ground when half the flowers are open.
- New growth after cutting will provide more flower stems all summer.
- Place cut stems in hot water.

Firethorn (Pyracantha)

- Evergreen shrub that's easy to grow, with orange or red berries.
- Choose cultivars for early or late blooming, berry color and hardiness to match your growing zone.
- Cut at least half the stems to stimulate next year's growth.

Flowering Quince (Chaenomelas)

- Extremely hardy shrub – one of the first to bloom each year.
- For blooms in January – harvest budded stems and force in greenhouse.
- Available in a wide variety of colors – from whites to reds.
- Harvest in season when flowers are in full bloom.
- Thornless varieties are easier to handle.

Forsythia

- Early blooming shrub produces yellow flowers from February to April.
- Can be forced up to six weeks early.
- Harvest just before buds open.
- Cutting stems close to ground will stimulate new growth.

Heavenly Bamboo (Nandina domestica)

- A multi-purpose plant that provides foliage used by florists as a filler in arrangements, flowers in spring, and berries in the fall.
- Not very cold-tolerant – check to make sure it's suited for your area.

Holly (Ilex)

- Evergreen shrub best known for its red berries.
- Be sure to plant both male and female plants to insure berries.
- Spiny leaves hard to handle.
- Deciduous variety "winterberry" does better in northern areas.

Hydrangea

- Grown both as a cut flower and for drying.
- H.paniculata "Grandiflora" a popular variety.
- Harvest when half the flowers are open.

- Does best in mild climates – check to be sure your climate zone is suitable.
- H.macrophylla a popular drying variety.

Lilac (Syringa)

- Prefers alkaline soil – add lime if your soil is acid.
- Harvest when almost in full bloom and place in warm water with floralife – out of the sun.
- Can be forced to bloom six weeks ahead of time.
- Sensitive to over-pruning; take out less than half of old branches at the end of blooming season.

Redbud (Cercis canadensis)

- This native of the Eastern U.S. is fast growing.
- Clusters of early spring flowers of white or pink.
- Harvest when half the flower buds have opened, and put the stems in water with Floralife.

Red Osier Dogwood (Cornus sericea)

- This native plant, when given plenty of water, grows like a weed.
- Bright red winter twigs can be cut and stored in water for months.
- Yellow twig dogwood is also popular.
- Cutting all new growth back each year stimulates next year's growth.

Viburnum

- Several deciduous species provide spring flowers.
- Growers can also harvest berries and foliage for fall sales.
- Preferred species include: Double life Viburnum (V.plicatum), European Cranberry and Snowball bush (V.opulus), Korean Spice Viburnum (V. carlesii) and Burkwood Viburnum (V.burkwoodii).

Weigela

- Masses of late spring and early summer flowers make up for short vase life.
- Cutting entire plant back halfway will produce an abundance of flowers through the next year.
- Many hybrid varieties to choose from for blooms ranging from white to ruby red.

Willow (Salix)

- Most popular sellers are: curly willow (S.matsudana) and pussy willow (S.discolor).
- Buy one "mother plant", as willows are easy to propagate from cuttings.
- Harvest pussy willows in spring when catkins are emerging.
- Harvest curly willow after leaves have fallen and stem color is most intense.

Growing Flower Bulbs

Flower bulbs can be one of the best crops for the specialty flower grower. Besides being easy to grow, most bulbs multiply rapidly with proper care. "Bulb" is a general term used to describe both true bulbs, such as daffodils and tulips, and other underground food storehouses called corms (Crocus), rhizomes (Iris) and tubers.

For the commercial grower, bulbs that are forced to flower out of season are especially profitable. "Forcing" simulates natural conditions to cause bulbs to bloom months before the normal cycle.

The secret to forcing is to plant early enough to allow the bulb to develop a sturdy root system. Popular flowers for forcing include:

- "Paperwhite" daffodil for Christmas.
- "February Gold" daffodil for January.
- "Olaf" tulip for Valentine's Day.
- "Peerless Pink" tulip for Mother's Day.
- "Anne Marie" hyacinth for Valentine's Day.
- "Grote Gele" Dutch crocus for January.

Best-Selling Flower Bulbs

Canna

These popular large perennials, with their lush tropical foliage and gladiolus-like flowers make borders and planting beds come alive with their vivid colors. Cannas also bloom all thru the summer until the first frost. Cannas prefer a fertile, well-drained loamy soil. Plant about two inches deep in a sunny location with a spacing of one to two feet between plants.

Harvest after the first frost, when the leaves die back. The cannas spread by underground runners, called rhizomes. Lift and divide the rhizomes, discarding old growth. Store over the winter in peat moss or dry sand.

Crocus

The crocus is the best-known springtime flowering bulb. Hardy in almost all areas, most bloom in early spring, but some species will bloom in the fall. The hybrids, also called Dutch Crocus, are the most vigorous and popular for forcing into early bloom in pots. The non-hybrids bloom earlier and have unusual coloration.

Crocus prefer sun or light shade, and a light, porous soil. Set the corms two to three inches deep and three inches apart. Crocus tend to multiply almost as fast as rabbits, but a commercial grower can accelerate the process even more by root division or by inducing lateral buds. Any good book on plant propagation can show you the specific methods.

Daffodils

This hardy perennial originated in Europe and has become one of the most popular bulbs, partly because of their virtual immunity to diseases and pests. Even gophers hate daffodil bulbs! Daffodils are excellent for naturalizing, with vigorous growth, long life and an abundance of flowers. All daffodils are members of the genus Narcissis, and are usually grouped into twelve divisions, according to their shape.

Daffodils are easy to grow, preferring a well-drained soil and full sun or semi-shade. Bulbs should be planted early in the fall, spaced about eight inches apart and four to six inches deep. They should be mulched in area with severe winters. Bulbs naturally divide in half each year, so to help the process along, you simply remove one half and plant it elsewhere.

Gladiolus

A popular cut flower, glads have an extremely wide color range, and bloom from spring to fall, depending on the time of planting. The newer varieties of garden gladiolus have spikes and will stand upright without staking. Glads prefer a rich sandy soil, full sun, and frequent watering. They develop up to fifty "cormels", which are miniature corms produced between the new corm and the dying old corm.

Collect the cormels when the corm is lifted from the ground before winter. Store them below 40 degrees in a dry, frost-free area with good air circulation. Soak cormels that have become dried out in tap water for a day before planting. Cormels will normally take two years to mature. Planting the first bulbs in early spring and then every week for a few weeks will provide blooms throughout the summer. Plant the corms about four times deeper than their height.

Iris

A large and diverse group of about two hundred species, varying in form, color, growing requirements and methods of propagation. The best-known groups are the crested, the beardless, and the bearded, all three spreading by rhizomes – underground runners. One variety, the roof iris, was traditionally planted in the thatched roofs of Japanese homes.

Iris must have a rich, well-drained soil, as it will not tolerate "wet feet" Planting depth is critical. The rhizomes should be barely covered with soil. Rhizomes should be planted between July and October and spaced about 12 to 18 inches apart. The rhizomes grow from the end with leaves. The best time to divide the rhizomes is just after flowering.

Hostas

Hostas are a hardy, broad-leaved member of the lily family that does well in either wet or dry conditions. For many hosta lovers, the leaves are more important than the flowers, with a wide variety of colors, textures and sizes. The entire plant dies back to the ground each year, then re-appears in the spring, with a dense growth that can shade out even the most determined weed.

Hostas prefer a loamy, moist soil, and partial to full shade to do well. You can propagate in early spring or fall by root division. Division stimulates plants, so cut the root crown in pieces and replant before the roots dry out. The size of the pieces will depend on how many developed shoots are on the crown, as each piece needs at least one shoot.

Hyacinth

This lovely flower originated in the Mediterranean area and is known for its delicate scent. The hyacinth is popular for forcing in the winter months. It must have well- drained soil to prevent bulb rot.

In northern climates, bulbs should be planted in September or October. In milder climates, plant in October through December. Set the bulbs as deep as their diameter, and six to twelve inches apart. Hyacinths normally multiply too shortly for commercial purposes, so artificial propagation must be used. These techniques are illustrated in most plant propagation books.

Lilies

One of the most varied garden plants, the lilies are often called "The Glories of the Garden". Their large clusters of vivid flowers bloom from July through September with a lovely fragrance. About sixty years ago, breeders developed many new hybrids which were healthier, hardier and easier to grow. As a result, it's now possible to grow healthy bulbs in large commercial quantities with a minimum of problems.

Lilies are generally easy to grow. They prefer a deep, well-drained soil with ample moisture. Planting in filtered sunlight brings out the colors and makes the blossoms last longer. Plant the bulbs four to eight inches deep, and twelve inches apart.

Tulips

The tulip was once a holy flower in Turkey and Iran, where it originated. The name comes from the Turkish word for turban. In the 17th century, during the great Dutch "tulip-mania", bulb prices spiraled up and up until a single bulb was worth its weight in gold. Fortunately for us, prices are now more reasonable, so everyone can enjoy the tulip rainbow of color.

Tulips always do best in a rich loam that's well-drained, and in full sun. Planting new bulbs six inches deep and six inches apart will insure both an ample supply of new bulblets, and excellent flowering quality for selling cut flowers. Shallow planting can lead to undersize bulbs and flowers the next season. To produce large bulbs for sale in quantity, you should lift, divide and store your bulbs in early summer. Use a garden fork and T.L.C. to avoid injuring the bulbs.

Marketing Flower Bulbs

Small-scale growers have found that quality bulbs at fair prices sell out quickly. Try farmer's markets and postcard ads on local bulletin boards. Be sure to mention your address and prices! Here are a few bulb-specific marketing tips:

- Grade your bulbs by size, and package in ventilated clear plastic bags, (you can use a paper punch to quickly make vents) as pre-packaged bulbs will sell faster.
- Label each bag with price, color and variety.
- Sell twelve large bulbs or eighteen medium bulbs for the same price.
- Have an instruction sheet for each customer on how to grow great flowers. A satisfied customer will come back for more bulbs next year – and the next.
- Offer packages of bulbs that grow and bloom in sequence all spring and summer.

- Give your customers a "baker's dozen" – an extra bulb with each dozen. Nothing pleases a customer more than an unexpected bonus.

- Sell forced-bulb plants early in the spring through local garden centers, florists and grocery stores.

- Sell your smaller bulbs by the pound to local gardeners who enjoy growing their own bulbs.

- Bulb fund-raisers. Pick your favorite local organization to sell bulbs as a fund raiser for a percentage of sales. One grower sells $30,000 worth of bulbs every year this way.

- If you decide to specialize in unique varieties, consider mail-order or internet sales. Try a small classified ad in national or regional gardening magazines.

Marketing Your Flowers

According to Paul Savage, a Northwest flower grower, "The common thread that runs between all the flower markets is quality. It's quality that determines if we sell our product at a profit. Quality brings repeat sales, and that's what we all need."

As a beginning grower, you'll need to study your potential markets to determine which approach is best for you. In addition, you'll need to study your competition to determine what's hot and what's not, prices of flowers and value-added products, and marketing techniques that work. In the resource section, you'll find a selection of organization and newsletters devoted to the floral world. Subscribe to at least one – you'll be repaid many times over in new ideas you can use and profit from.

Pricing

A common mistake of new growers is pricing their flowers and value-added products too low. To prevent that mistake, it's important to know how much your flowers are worth. The best way for most growers to find out is to stay informed of market prices, so you'll be able to set prices to the "market".

The market for flowers is just as dynamic as any other commodities market, changing daily in response to supply and demand, weather conditions and a host of other factors.

You'll also need to tailor your individual pricing to your primary sales efforts. For example, if you're selling your flowers mostly by the bunch or bouquet at retail farmer's markets, just keeping an eye on what others are charging should do.

If you're selling by the stem to wholesale customers, such as florists, accurate pricing information is even more important. Many retail florists are willing to share their wholesale price lists with local growers, once you get to know each other, and that can be quite helpful.

Top Markets for Your Flowers

Customers for flowers fall into three main areas: direct retail sales, direct sales to retailers, and wholesale sales. Within these three categories, there are several unique markets for your flowers. Let's take a closer look at each market.

Direct Retail Sales

Selling your flowers direct to the consumer will produce the highest profits for you. Another advantage is that you get your money now- no waiting 30-60 days for a check, and no collection problems. Another advantage of direct retail sales is that because your volume is lower than that of a large wholesale grower, you'll need less land (and hired help) for your growing operation.

Selling direct also allows you to mix your "hot" sellers and your slow sellers in bunches or assortments so you can count on selling most of what you grow. The flip side? Direct retail sales take more time – you'll spend a lot of time talking to your customers and away from your garden. Here are six proven methods for direct retail sales:

Farmer's Markets

Farmer's Markets are growing like weeds! According to the USDA, the number of farmer's markets has been increasing 10% or more each year.

They can be an excellent way for you to sell your flowers. Even if you don't have a booth or stall when you're starting out, you can find someone that is selling non- competing products to share space with.

One successful flower grower displays a large bouquet of flowers at each farmer's market that is the prize in a regular drawing. Any customer can fill out an entry card for the drawing. This provides the grower with a free mailing list of customers.

She then mails a simple one-page sales flyer to her list several times a year, inviting them to her garden for a "private" Saturday sale. She has as much business as she wants, selling just one day a week.

Successful sellers at Farmer's Markets claim there are only three "secrets" to making money with your booth or display.

- **First** – make sure that the quality of your flowers is the very best. If it doesn't look great, don't try to sell it.
- **Next** – your prices must be fair, but not so low that they undercut the other sellers. Many growers charge more on purpose, to make shoppers think their flowers must be higher quality!
- **Last** – An attractive display enhances your flowers and attracts customers. Try three or four levels for your display so your flowers are easy to see. Signs and prices should be attractive, and large enough to read easily.

If the market does not provide booths, a canopy is handy for both shade and shelter. Flowers look better out of the hot sun – and so do vendors! Look for basic affordable canopies at stores like Costco, Target or Home Depot, or ask other market vendors.

Roadside Stands

Link up with another grower in your area who already has a roadside stand. You'll both benefit with increased sales, because produce and flowers are a natural combination. You can also set up a small stand of your own with an "honor" pay box.

In many areas, the local Chamber of Commerce or tourist bureau publishes a map or directory to help visitors locate all the roadside stands. Be sure you're on the map!

Grower Direct

Many growers have a "wholesale day" one Saturday morning a month. Run a classified ad in your local newspaper in the week preceding the sale day. Your ad might read:

Fresh Flowers – Wholesale Prices Public Welcome – 123 Smith Road Saturday Only 9 a.m. – 2 p.m.

As one grower who uses this approach exclusively said, "make sure you have some extra sales help, because this one really does work." Be sure that everything is tagged before the sale so you'll be free to help customers. A simple, effective pricing system uses color-coded stickers. Group all your bunched flowers in three or four price categories, each with its own color code.

A simple sign, showing the colors and the price per bunch is all you'll need. Be sure to ask all purchasers if they would like to sign up for your "preferred customer" mailing list for announcements of future sales, or try a drawing, as mentioned earlier.

Hotels and Restaurants

Upscale hotels are steady buyers of fresh cut flowers and arrangements. Many more "budget" hotels and motels would be receptive to using bouquets of dried flowers, replaced every month or so. The cost is much less than using fresh cut bouquets, which have to be replaced much more frequently.

Restaurants in your area can be your best customers, buying fresh cuts to decorate their tables in season, then switching to everlastings in the off-season. In addition many restaurants use a large floral arrangement near the entry that is changed weekly.

Subscription Sales

Sally Gardner may have created the ultimate floral business. She works one day a week, and every flower is presold !

According to Gardner, there's room for a similar floral subscription business in almost every town, large or small. Gardner's floral service delivers flower bouquets to offices and homes in her California community at the beginning of every week According to one of her satisfied customers,

> *"Flowers cheer the office up. It's colorful, it's alive, and you don't have to dust it!"*

When Gardner started her business, her goal was to avoid waste and order only what the customer would pay for, and provide a steady income. Her model was a job she'd had as a teenager – a newspaper route. Patterned after her paper route, her customers buy flower subscriptions on a monthly basis, paying from $12 to $150 each week, depending on how many bouquets they order.

According to Gardner: "People buy subscriptions so you have guaranteed sales. There's no spoilage or waste. You know how much your costs are, and what you're going to make."

Each Monday, seasonal cut flowers are used to design three bouquet sizes, desktop, midAsize, and lobby. The smaller bouquets include 10 – 15 stems, and the largest 15 – 18 stems, with different colors and varieties each week. Bouquets range in price from $12 to $20 per week and are delivered in a plastic sleeve. Customers range from homes to doctor's offices to corporate headquarters.

Mail-Order Sales

Many growers have been successful selling their dried flowers, arrangements and value-added products such as wreaths by mail. Some growers sell through major catalogs, such as Smith-Hawken. Others use classified ads in floral trade publications – both local and national– and crafts magazines.

Ralph Cramer, a Pennsylvania grower, had this to say about classified ads: "After I wasted money on a high-priced ad in Country Living that was only one inch high, I asked a friend who was in advertising for some free advice. She said I should advertise in as many cheap classified columns as I could, with the same exact words in each ad.

The purpose is to create a sense of familiarity when your potential customers see your ad over and over. She was right – I had a lot of people I met later tell me they saw my ads "everywhere."

Direct Sales to Retailers

If your goal is to increase your volume and grow more, you'll want to expand your markets to include retailers, such as antique stores, florists, food co-ops, grocery stores and supermarkets and gift and craft shops.

To get started in this area, talk to retailers who may be interested in stocking your flowers or value-added floral products. Find out what they are interested in buying – bunches or bouquets, for example, and the quantity they might need.

Here's where you'll need to do some comparison shopping to find out what others are charging, and what seems to be selling well in the different retail outlets. Do this research first, so when it's time to talk prices with your potential customers, you'll have some solid numbers. Keep in mind that retailers will mark up your prices 40%-50% to arrive at a retail price.

Bouquets means Big Bucks for Flower Farmers

Frank and Pamela Arnosky, Texas flower farmers, have had great success making and selling mixed floral bouquets, which they call Texas Garden Bouquets at a variety of outlets such as supermarkets and farmer's markets. Selling over 1,000 bouquets on Mother's Day week, they say the demand is only limited by what they can physically produce.

They plant a variety of flowers with bouquets in mind, then pick the flowers twice a week when the blooms are ready. They try for 7 varieties of flowers, and around 15 stems per bouquet. A "Big" flower, like a sunflower or gladiola is the focus of the bouquet, surrounded by less showy flowers and "filler" flowers like solidago and gypsophilia.

Customers who are antique shopping are also potential customers for old-fashioned everlasting bouquets, arrangements and wreaths. One shop owner was having trouble selling a collection of antique glass vases until she added a small bouquet of everlastings to each one and doubled the price. The result – three dozen sold in a month.

Florists

Some growers prefer dealing with a few regular customers to allow them to spend more time growing and less time selling. Florists are an ideal market for this type of grower, as a few retail florists can provide a good income for the growers who can supply what they need.

To sell to retail florists, talk to a few shop owners to find out the flowers and colors are in demand, the quantity they use, and how much they are paying. Explain that you are just getting started and want to grow flowers that are in demand.

Be sure to mention, as a selling point, that, as a local grower, you can supply them with fresher flowers, with no shipping damage (a common problem when buying flowers from a distant source). If you have the skills, you can also supply them with value- added products, such as wreaths. When you've begun to harvest your flowers, take samples to all the florists you've contacted so they can see the quality and colors of your crop.

Food Co-Ops

Our local food co-op is supplied by a backyard grower who has filled her tiny city lot with flower beds. Driving down her street, you can spot her garden a block away! She supplies fresh bouquets in season and everlasting bouquets out of season. Her only outlet – by choice – is the food co-op, yet it provides her with a tidy income.

Grocery Stores and Supermarkets

According to a recent survey, consumers are buying less from traditional florists and more from supermarket floral departments. The same survey found that 90% of supermarkets regularly sell flowers. This is a large potential market for the serious grower.

You'll need to have a large volume of flowers to sell to supermarkets, less to the smaller grocery stores. Do some comparison shopping and find out what they are currently selling, and the prices they're charging. Like other retailers, a 40-50% markup to retail is normal.

Gift and Craft Shops

If you are doing mixed collections, bouquets, arrangements, wreaths and other decorative items, gift and craft shops can be a natural outlet for you. Shop around to see what they are now stocking. Until you are well-established, you may need to place your everlastings and value-added products on consignment.

This arrangement means the shop owner doesn't have to pay up-front and worry whether the product will sell, so they'll be more likely to say yes to you than if you require immediate payment. Consignment sales are typically made at a 25-35% discount, rather than the usual 40-50%, because of the deferred payment. It can be a "win – win" for both parties. Crafters buy everlastings to make their own wreaths, bouquets and other decorative items. Selling your everlastings through a craft shop gives you exposure to a new market.

Wholesalers

If you're ready to expand your volume, and focus more on growing than selling, wholesalers can help you move your flowers in large quantities. Your profit is the lowest of all sales approaches. Wholesale florists usually sell only to retail florists, often just in their geographic area. Many prefer not to deal with smaller growers, and buy much of their stock from cheaper overseas sources. If you grow something unique, they'll buy it from you. But be prepared for large orders and slim profits.

Value-Added Products

If you have a talent for floral design, consider selling value-added products such as bouquets, arrangements and wreaths. You can easily turn $5 worth of plant material into as much as $50 worth of floral products.

Adding value works especially well with everlastings, as they'll look terrific for months – even years with no watering or care. This makes them appealing to businesses that want the decorative effect of flowers without the on-going expense or bother. Possible customers include professional offices (doctors, dentists, lawyers), banks, restaurants, hotels, antique shops, gift shops and bookstores.

Speaking of value-added products…consider making your own floral insecticide! Pyrethrum is a botanical insecticide produced from Chrysanthemum plants (Chrysanthemum cinerariaefolium).

Classes

Many growers find classes and workshops are a profitable addition to growing flowers. If you're good at wreath making or floral arrangements, why not consider sharing your skills and knowledge with others? Growers who do workshops and classes can host them at home, or work through community sponsors such as the local Parks and Recreation Department or Community College. One grower holds her classes in the back room of a craft supply shop, with the shop providing free space and advertising in return for the opportunity to sell more craft supplies.

CHAPTER 9

Growing Herbs

Herbs have been used in cooking, medicine and cosmetics for thousands of years. Now, herbs are being rediscovered, as people around the globe seek a healthier and more natural lifestyle. Herbs also provide a link to our past – a time when the pace was slower, things were simpler and almost everyone had a backyard herb garden.

Herbal use has grown dramatically in recent years. Today, you'll find cooks using more fresh herbs. New medical research has shown many herbs can be useful as healthy alternatives to expensive drugs. In Germany, for example, doctors write seven times as many prescriptions for St. John's Wort as for Prozac when treating patients for depression! Walk into almost any retail store, and you'll find herbs used in an amazing variety of products – soaps, candles, teas, potpourris, medicines, and bath oils.

Although Europeans use almost four times more cooking herbs than we Americans, this is changing fast, as cooks discover the benefits of cooking with fresh herbs. Thanks to the influence of cooking magazines, TV cooking shows, and a growing level of culinary awareness, more and more consumers are buying potted herbs to grow and use at home.

Europeans also use more herbs for medicinal purposes than Americans. In Germany, a medical council called "Commission E" reviews herbs for safety and effectiveness, and its recommendations are used by doctors throughout Europe, and by a growing number of doctors in North America as well.

It's easy for a newcomer to the herb business to get overwhelmed by all the choices. You can focus on just growing herbal plants, making herbal products or decorations, grow herbs for the fresh-cut market, grow and dry herbs, sell to the wholesale and bulk herb buyers – the list goes on!

It's important for newcomers to find a niche that fits both their experience level, skills and the local market. Starting a backyard herb nursery can be a wonderful way for herbal beginners to turn their love of plants and gardening into cash. It's one of the best ways to "bootstrap" a few hundred dollars into a good part-time or full-time income. In this chapter, you'll learn how to grow and market the ten most popular culinary and the ten most popular medicinal herbs, using potted plants as your special "niche."

The secret to making good money with a backyard herb nursery is to specialize in high demand popular plants that can be container grown to save space, time and water. Just one small backyard mini-greenhouse (also called a "hoop house") with 100 square feet of growing space will hold 400 – 6-inch potted herb plants with a retail value of over $2400. One grower, limited to a fifty-foot wide backyard, was able to set up eight of these growing beds, earning over $20,000 in three months.

In addition to selling potted herb plants, you'll learn about "value-added" herb products, such as herbal pet products, herbal windowsill gardens, and dream pillows to produce sales even after the selling season for potted plants is over.

Remember to start small and learn from your growing and marketing successes and mistakes. After you've grown the basic herbs for a season or two, you'll be better equipped to expand into other herbs or other varieties of the same herbs.

Start a second batch of basil seeds every two or three weeks to provide fresh plants during the selling season. Basil will be your best-selling herb, so you'll need lots of it.

Top Ten Culinary Herbs

CHIVES (Allium schoenoprasum) This standard chive is better for the market grower than the more exotic varieties such as garlic chives. Chives do better in clumps, so you'll want to start the seeds in a cluster of several seeds. Mist the seeds every day until they germinate. After about a week, the plants will germinate.

Now you can start watering the plants, being careful to water only the base of the plants. (A morning watering is best for almost all herb plants) Two weeks after sprouts appear, fertilize with liquid fish fertilizer.

Chives are quite hardy, so you can safely set them out in the growing bed in cooler weather.

CILANTRO (Coriandrum sativum) The leafy parts of this annual herb are known as cilantro, while the seeds are called coriander. Cilantro is a popular culinary herb that also has medicinal properties, as it is widely used to maintain digestive health. It's a popular herb at the Saturday market.

Cilantro prefers moist soil and a cool growing climate – too hot and it will bolt. Put two seeds in each plug, lightly misting until the plants sprout. A weekly boost of liquid fish fertilizer will help the plants reach "ready-to- sell" stage sooner. Park Seed (www.parkseed.com) has a variety, "Delfino", that is slow to bolt.

MARJORAM (Marjorana hortensis) Sweet marjoram is a herb with a delicate flavor similar to oregano. Of the dozens of varieties available, the sweet variety is the most popular for culinary use, including the edible flowers. Calming and soothing, it's also used in aromatherapy.

Put two or three seeds in each plug, then mist until they sprout. Thin to the best plant and give it a boost of liquid fish fertilizer. Pinch out the tops after the plant has grown a bit to encourage bushing out.

OREGANO (Origanum) Oregano is almost as important as tomatoes in Italian cooking. This popular herb offers an unforgettable taste and aroma. A hardy perennial from the marjoram family, oregano is also used as a garnish for stews, gravies and soups.

The best oregano variety for culinary use is called Greek oregano. Many growers have had success offering an "Italian

Herb" combo of oregano, rosemary and sage. Price the combo at 10 percent less that the price of three individual pots, and you'll sell lots of them!

MINT (Mentha) The hardy mint family, including applemint, chocolate mint, orange mint, spearmint and peppermint, are vigorous plants, and tolerate shady spots and cold weather well. Because of its vigor, it can be harvested as soon as it gets six inches high, by pinching off the tops as the plant grows.

The mints are a favorite flavoring for teas, jellies and candies. Chocolate mint is a popular seller at Saturday markets, with its unusual coloration. The large commercial growers harvest peppermint and spearmint for their oil. One member of the mint family, pennyroyal, is used in sachets to repel moths and added to dog beds to discourage fleas.

PARSLEY (Petroselinium) Parsley is so well known that it is often considered more a vegetable than a herb. The ancient Greeks wove it into victory crowns for the athletic games and fed it to racehorses to make them run faster.

Today, parsley is widely used as a decorative herb, in bouquet garni, and in soups, stews, sauces and stuffing. The leaves are known as a breath sweetener and rich in vitamins and minerals. The flat-leaf varieties are more nutritious than the curly types and sell out faster at the market.

ROSEMARY (Rosemarinus officinalis) This evergreen plant in native to the Mediterranean region, where it can reach a height of 6-feet and live as long as 20 years. Rosemary is one of the most popular culinary herbs and is often used as an insect repellant.

SAGE (Salvia officinalis) Garden sage is a hardy perennial that's a member of the mint family. There are several varieties available, but the most commonly grown is S. officinalis, with purple flowers. Sage is an important culinary herb, widely used in stuffings, soups, gravies, meats, eggs and sausage. Sage jelly has a uniquely delicious flavor.

TARRAGON (Artemesia dracunculus) Hippocrates, the "father of medicine", was prescribing tarragon for a variety of ailments over two thousand years ago. In the Middle Ages, pilgrims put sprigs of tarragon in their shoes for increased endurance on their journey.

Today, this hardy perennial is one of the most popular culinary herbs. It enhances the flavors of other herbs and gives a unique flavor to egg and fish dishes, salads and sauces. Of all the herb vinegars, none is better known than tarragon vinegar. Tarragon is also an essential ingredient in tartar sauce and sauce bernaise.

The tarragon sold as a culinary herb is French tarragon, which must be grown from cuttings or purchased plants. Buy a few plants, and propagate your own tarragon from stem cuttings of new growth in the spring

THYME (Thymus vulgaris) Another member of the mint family, thyme has dozens of variations in shape, texture and flavor. Common thyme is the most widely used culinary variety, and is sometimes also called Garden thyme, English thyme or French thyme. Lemon thyme is a popular seller at the Saturday market.

Because thyme keeps its aroma well when dried, it is an excellent winter herb for flavoring bouquet garni, soups and stews. Thyme is often used as a ground cover in orchards to attract bees for pollination.

Top Ten Medicinal Herbs

CALENDULA (Calendula officinalis) King Henry VIII of England loved colored food, and his cooks often used calendula flowers to season his meals, hence the nickname "pot marigold". Calendula is often used in skin preparations, and also for digestive concerns.

The flowers can easily be made into tinctures, ointments and salves, or used as a foot soak or bath herb. To improve its potency as a medicinal herb, grow varieties with a high resin content, such as "Resina", available from Johnny's Seeds.

This is one of the easiest medicinal herbs to grow. The flowers are harvested before the plant starts putting energy into seed making, to maximize the resin content.

CATNIP (Nepeta cataria) This pet favorite acts as a stimulant on cats, but as a soothing sedative for people. In addition, it can provide pain and stress relief and help with cold and flu symptoms.

In the value-added chapter, you'll learn how to make "cat-er-pillows", a must have for every cat owner. Catnip is used in medicinal tinctures, salves and foot soaks. It's also a popular ingredient in dream pillows. A simple display of *caterpillows* next to your potted catnip plants will often double sales, as customers realize they can make their own.

CHAMOMILE (Matricaria recutita) German chamomile is the variety to grow, producing harvestable flowers in just over two months. It's easy to grow, and fast to produce a saleable potted plant. You'll have better luck with early plantings, as it tends to bolt in the hot summer.

The fresh picked flowers make a soothing tea, and chamomile has long been valued as a medicinal plant in Europe, where it is used as a digestive, calming and sleep aid in a variety of forms.

ECHINACEA (Echinacea augustifolia, Echinacea purpurea)

This is a high demand herb that sells well as a potted plant. It stimulates the immune system, and is often used for colds and flu, respiratory and skin conditions. Although the whole plant – roots, leaves and flowers – is typically used in crafting herbal products, the flowers and leaves are more commonly used in Europe.

This is fortunate for beginning growers, as the flowers and leaves can be harvested in the first and second year, while the roots take longer to mature. Echinacea augustifolia is the native plant that has traditionally been harvested in the wild, but now seeds are readily available, including a "primed" seed from Johnny's Seeds that germinates quickly and uniformly.

LAVENDER (Lavender augustifolia) Lavender has been called the "Swiss army knife" of herbs because it has so many uses. Everyone loves the fragrant flowers, but not everyone knows that the leaves, stems and flowers are all medicinally useful for skin care, women's and children's health, nervous system conditions and pain relief.

The essential oil extracted from lavender is one of the top ten in the fragrance industry, and anyone with a plant or two at home can easily use the same essential oil simply by making an infusion or tincture. Lavender is also widely used for foot soaks, bath soaks and for sleep/dream pillows.

LEMON BALM (Melissa officinalis) This popular herb is vigorous and easy to grow. The strongly scented leaves are a popular tea herb, beneficial to the digestive tract, and an immune booster. It's also considered a great stress reducer. The dried leaves of lemon balm are perfect for dream pillows as well. Trimming the plant back after flowering will encourage even more leaf production.

LEMON VERBENA (Aloysia triphylla) The leaves of this popular herb, which contain an abundance of volatile oils, make a wonderful tea. For maximum potency and flavor, harvest the leaves just before using them whenever possible. The leaves can also be dried for future tea making. Lemon verbena tea is used for calming, as a digestive aid and as a sleep aid.

Lemon verbena is best propagated from softwood stem cuttings rather than from seed. Buy a plant or two, then take cuttings from the new softwood. Use a rooting hormone and stick the cuttings to propagate new plants. It is a tender plant, so make sure it has protection in colder weather.

MARSHMALLOW (Althaea officinalis) In the nineteenth century, a sugary treat was actually made from the roots of this plant, so now you know where the real campfire treat originated. This herb is good for coughs and bronchitis, the digestive tract and many skin conditions. A marshmallow tea is useful during the cold and flu season.

The roots, leaves and flowers are all used in medicinal preparations. As a pot herb, the leaves can be harvested as needed for use.

MONARDA (Monarda didyma, Monarda fistulosa) This tasty herb is also known as Bergamot (M. fistulosa), and Bee balm (M. didyma). If you've ever enjoyed a cup of Earl Grey tea, thank bergamot for the distinct flavor. Cooks often substitute fresh monarda leaves for Greek oregano.

Monarda is often used for digestive and respiratory ailments, as well as winter ailments, such as colds.

MULLEIN (Verbascum thapsus) This easy to grow herb is a vigorous grower, producing an abundance of downy gray-green leaves, which are used for the respiratory tract and skin. The flowers can be used in an infused oil to treat earache. Be careful not to overwater mullein, as it prefers a dry, well-drained soil.

ST JOHN'S WORT (Hypericum perforatum) Mention St. John's wort, and most folks immediately think "herbal prozac." But in addition to its mood altering abilities, St John's wort is valued for immune support, cold and flu prevention and – as a salve – a skin treatment.

The healing ingredient in St. John's wort, hypericin, is found in the flowering tops and not other parts of the plant. Wait until the plant is in full bloom before harvesting to get the full healing benefits.

STEVIA (Stevia rebaudiana) The leaves and flowers of this herb are very sweet, which is why stevia is widely used as a sweetener. It's also been used to heal cuts and wounds with less scarring, improve digestion, help with skin conditions such as acne, eczema and dermatitis, reduce plaque and inhibit tooth decay and even reduce the desire for alcohol.

No wonder stevia is such a popular herb! It's been used as a sweetener by South American natives for centuries. As Stevia is a heat-loving plant, northern growers will need to protect it from colder temperatures.

Herbal Teas & Infusions

You will sell many more herb plants if your customers learn about the many benefits herbs offer. Herbal teas are growing in popularity, especially the medicinal teas, also called infusions. The main difference between tea and an infusion is the length of time the herbs are steeped. While most teas are steeped for about five minutes, an infusion is typically steeped for 20-30 minutes in a closed jar to create a stronger beverage.

Most teas and infusions use leaves and flowers, with a few made from plant roots. Almost everyone has enjoyed mint tea, which can be made with the fresh or dried leaves of any plant in the mint family, including catnip. Here's a list of the herbs covered in this guide that are ideal for teas and infusions:

- Calendula … Use the flowers.
- Catnip … Use the leaves.
- Chamomile … Use the flowers.
- Echinacea … Use the flowers.
- Lemon Balm … Use the leaves.
- Lemon Verbena … Use the leaves.
- Marshmallow … Use the leaves.
- Mint family … Use the leaves.
- Mullein … Use the leaves.
- Monarda … Use the leaves.

Growing Potted Herbs

To keep startup costs low yet provide the best growing environment for healthy herb plants, a mini-greenhouse is ideal. It can be built in any length to accommodate the space you have available, but the width should be 40 inches or less to allow easy access to both sides of the growing area.

Using the "Quick Hoop" system developed by Johnny's Seeds, you can build mini greenhouses on your raised beds to extend the growing season and protect your plants from wind and predators. The cost of the mini greenhouses is low, compared to the benefits, and most growers find they repay the cost in just a season. You'll find several videos at their website that explain how to build and use them.

How many potted plants can you grow in a 30-foot raised bed? Using a standard 6-inch diameter pot, you'll have room for about 400 plants. Most growers find that customers prefer a larger plant in a larger pot and are willing to pay a premium price for it. In addition, by using a larger pot, you distinguish your plants from the smaller ones available everywhere else.

Commercial herb growers have found that a prepared growing soil blend works best for production of herb plants. Here's a recipe for enough growing mix to fill 400 six - inch pots:

- 8 cubic feet washed sand
- 8 cubic feet topsoil
- 12 cubic feet peat moss
- 4 cubic feet perlite
- 10 pounds dolomite lime
- 10 pounds dry organic fertilizer

Most small - scale growers will find it easiest to mix the blend in small batches in a wheelbarrow, then fill the 6-inch pots directly from the wheelbarrow.

Herb Growing Tips

You should only use organic fertilizers to grow your herbs – here's why. Chemical fertilizers stimulate leaf growth but weaken the plants and make them prone to disease and insect damage. Organic fertilizers produce a steady, less stressed growth rate, which results in healthier herbs.

Every week or so during the growing season, apply liquid seaweed or liquid fish emulsion as a foliar spray. This will provide just the right amount of nutrients, and the foliar spraying allows the plants to make use of the nutrients immediately.

Read the seed packets to determine if a herb needs to be started indoors to insure good germination and protect it from cold weather. If so, set up a simple grow light in a warm area. An inexpensive 48 inch two or four bulb fluorescent or LED fixture with full spectrum bulbs will work well.

You can double your plant production with plugs and plug trays. Plug trays allow you to start hundreds of herb plants indoors, then transplant them to larger pots outdoors when they are ready. This allows you to maintain a rotation of plants, so you can have more than one batch of popular herbs, basil for example, in production. The best plug tray system for most herb growers is the Speedling plug trays, and the 200-plug size works well for herbs. You can learn more, or order them, from www.groworganic.com.

Because most herbs are soft-stemmed plants, they can be prone to fungi diseases. To avoid fungi diseases, give your plants plenty of light, dry conditions and air circulation.

Using a prepared soil mix will improve drainage. Water your plants only when they need it. To accomplish this, do your watering in the mornings, and avoid watering later in the day, or on damp days.

Raising the plastic cover on both ends of the hoop house tunnel and in the middle should provide good air circulation during the day. If not, set an inexpensive box fan at one or both ends to move the air, or raise the plastic covering on one side of the hoop house.

Because most herbs are soft-stemmed plants, they can be prone to fungi diseases. To avoid fungi diseases, give your plants plenty of light, dry conditions and air circulation.

Using a prepared soil mix will improve drainage. Water your plants only when they need it. To accomplish this, do your watering in the mornings, and avoid watering later in the day, or on damp days.

Make sure your growing location gets as much sun as possible. If a tree or building will shade the hoop house, try to locate it in a better place. Too much shade will reduce your plant growth rate dramatically.

Many beginning growers try to economize by using assorted recycled pots to grow herbs. Don't do it. Buy new pots – the wholesale cost is very reasonable. Pick a size – 6 inch, for example, and stick to it. Also be sure to buy trays that fit your choice of pots when you buy so you can easily transport your herb plants to Saturday market. The trays will prevent tip-overs and damaged plants.

Keep a "growing diary" with information about which varieties were planted, the seed source, germination rates, pest problems, size of plants, popularity at the market and so on. This information is valuable, as it allows you to improve your growing and marketing skills each year based on what you learn.

There are lots of sources for herb seeds. An internet search will produce dozens of results for any herb. Most growers will find everything they want at Johnny's Seeds (www.johnnyseeds.com) They have been selling seeds to small commercial growers for over 30 years. They carry most of the herbs mentioned in this guide, including "primed" seeds for varieties that are difficult to germinate.

Richter's (www.richters.com) is another great source for herbs. In business for over 40 years, they stock seeds for hundreds of common and unusual herbs. The "Pro Grower" section of their web site contains very detailed and helpful growing information (Click on "Grower Zone") and resources on the most popular herbs.

Raising the plastic cover on both ends of the hoop house tunnel and in the middle should provide good air circulation during the day. If not, set an inexpensive box fan at one or both ends to move the air, or raise the plastic covering on one side of the hoop house.

Hang yellow sticky cards to catch insects – either in your hoophouse or nearby. If you are catching a lot, it's a good early warning of an insect problem that may call for insecticide use. There are many effective organic insecticides available, so there's no need to use toxic chemicals on your herb plants. Visit www.arbico-organics.com to learn more about organic insecticides. Their web site has a handy "pest problem solver guide" to help you.

Grower Success Story

After ten years in the landscaping business, Barbara Patterson began producing her own potted herb plants. Rather than using the traditional 3-inch and 4-inch pots, she tried using a larger 6-inch pot. According to Barbara: "If you stay a little different, you remove yourself from the competitive market. A larger potted plant holds up better than the smaller plants, and produces a heavier root system, which keeps the customers more satisfied. The smaller potted plants just don't have the same survival as the larger plants."

To get a full looking pot, she usually puts two or three plants in each pot, rather than a single plant. This helps convince customers that their premium plants are worth top dollar. Thanks to those premium plants, Barbara seldom has to advertise, relying instead on happy customers to tell their friends.

Selling Potted Herbs

Most growers will make more money selling their potted herbs directly to the public. You'll get top dollar for your plants, and unlike selling wholesale, you'll get paid when the customer buys the plant. The four best ways to sell retail – aside from opening a store – are to:

SELL DIRECT. Check with your local authorities to determine if you can sell direct from your backyard garden. Most small growers who sell out of their home garden have limited hours – Saturdays only, for example.

If you choose to sell direct, try an ad in your local classified paper, such as the "Penny Saver or "Little Nickel", or even the internet classifieds such as Craigslist.com or Backpage.com. You can also post flyers and cards anywhere there is a bulletin board.

What if your local regulations don't permit regular retail sales. Try a garage sale or tag sale, which are allowed almost everywhere. Be specific in your garage sale ad, so everyone reading your ad will know that you're just selling potted herbs.

Many herb growers have a "wholesale day" one Saturday a month. Run a classified ad in your local paper in the week preceding the sale day. Your ad might read:

Buy Grower Direct !
Potted Culinary & Medicinal Herbs – Wholesale Prices Public
Welcome – 123 Smith Road Saturday Only 9 am to 2 pm

To encourage customers to buy more to save more, make up a price card for your "wholesale day" as follows:

Wholesale Pricing
Retail $5.95 / plant
1 plant = 20% discount
2-3 plants = 25% discount
4 or more plants = 30% discount

ROADSIDE STAND. Link up with a vegetable or flower grower in your area who already operates a roadside stand. You'll both benefit with increased sales, because produce or flowers and herbs are a natural combination. In many areas, the chamber of commerce or tourist bureau publishes a map or directory to help visitors locate roadside stands. Be sure you're on the map!

ORGANIZE A FUNDRAISER. Many herb growers work with their favorite charities, church groups or non-profits, doing a Saturday sale to raise money. You'll have plenty of help from volunteers, and a portion of your sales will go to your favorite good cause.

Several growers have reported that they can charge a bit more, as customers who buy at a fund raiser are not too "price-sensitive." Donating anywhere from 25 to 40 percent of gross sales is a typical split.

FARMER'S MARKET. A farmer's market can be a great way to sell your plants without having customers come to your home, You will pay a small fee for the space, but in return, you'll have lots of potential customers. Before you set up at a farmer's market, price shop local retailers that carry potted herbs, to make sure your prices are competitive. Pay particular attention to the pot sizes, and don't be afraid to charge more if you're selling a bigger, better or unique herb.

Farmer's markets are an excellent place to make contact with future customers, so pass out flyers and business cards to all who stop by, even if they don't buy today. Think of it as "planting the seeds" of future business.

Farmer's Market Selling Tips

PRICING. Growers like farmer's markets because they can keep the full retail price. As a new grower, it can be tempting to sell your herbs too cheaply. Don't do it! Old hands at the market know that they can do well with seemingly high prices. Remember the old expression: *"You get what you pay for."* Most shoppers will assume that if your prices are lower that something is wrong or inferior about your plants. If you have high quality plants, and charge more for them, shoppers will think your plants are above average and line up to buy from you!

DISPLAYS. If there's no shade where you'll be setting up, be sure to invest in a shade canopy, both for plants and people. You can find these at most retailers, like Target, WalMart or Home Depot, or go direct to the manufacturer at: www.ezupdirect.com. Keep your displays shallow so customers can reach the plants in the back. A folding table is usually 30 inches deep – ideal for displaying potted plants. Some growers prefer a stepped display, with three or more shelves, but make sure it is easy to set up and pack, and tip- resistant.

SIGNS. Make sure your signs are easy to read. Include the plant name and a price. People don't like to ask prices, so make sure yours are large and visible. An educational sign, laminated in plastic to prevent rain damage, next to each variety of herb, will help sell herbs. Mention how large the herb plant grows, what part of the plant is used, the culinary and medicinal uses for the plan, and growing/harvesting/drying tips.

MONEY. It's safer to wear a money apron, as it allows you to move around easily without having to keep an eye on a money box.

EDUCATION. Customers are thirsty for knowledge about herbs, and the more you share your knowledge, the more plants you will sell. Tell customers about the varieties of herbs you sell, tell them how to use and care for the plants, and pass out a simple printed handout with a list of all your herbs, together with as much useful information as you can fit on it. *(Hint – try an 8-1/2 x 11 sheet folded in half to make a four page "brochure".)* Connect to your customers and listen to them as well. Are they asking for a herb you don't have? Maybe you can supply it next year.

Value-Added Herb Products

Potted herb growers are finding that it's almost as easy to sell a "theme" collection of potted herbs as it is one plant. Several growers have made up simple wooden trays, large enough to hold three or four potted herb plants. The tray, made from scrap lumber, takes about ten minutes to assemble. Of course, a tray is not necessary to sell the herb collections, but it helps. A simple sign will do the trick as well. Here are some grower- tested combinations to get you started:

- **PASTA MINI-GARDEN.** Basil, Oregano & Rosemary.
- **ITALIAN HERB GARDEN.** Oregano, Rosemary & Sage.
- **FRENCH HERB GARDEN.** Lavender, Rosemary, Tarragon & Thyme.
- **WINDOWSILL HERB GARDEN.** Customer's choice of three herbs.
- **PERENNIAL HERB GARDEN.** Greek Oregano, English Thyme, English Mint & French Tarragon.
- **CITRUS HERB GARDEN.** Lemon Balm, Lemon Verbena, Lemon Mint & Lemon Thyme.
- **TEA TIME HERB GARDEN.** Lemon Verbena, Lemon Balm, Mint & Chamomile.
- **INSOMNIAC'S HERB GARDEN.** German Chamomile, Lemon Balm and Catnip.

HERBAL TEAS. Many herb growers also grow and dry their own herbal teas and blends. The teas are an excellent way to cross-sell plants, as customers can buy an ounce or two of tea to try before buying plants, and customers who buy plants don't have to wait for their plants to grow before enjoying a cup of herbal tea.

CAT-ER-PILLOW. This one drives cats crazy. One herb grower has had great success with catnip-filled pillows for cats that are sold at a variety of stores, street fairs, and church fundraisers. It's quite simple – a mini-pillow made from fabric scraps, filled with freshly dried catnip and sewn shut.

DREAM PILLOWS. For centuries, people have used herb blends to influence their dreams. Just as certain common fragrances – baking bread or lilacs in bloom, for example – evoke pleasant memories, herbs can do the same while we sleep. One herb grower has revived this tradition with new herbal blends, instruction books, and kits to mass-produce dream pillows.

His two most popular dream pillow herb blends are: *Pleasant Dreams,* a herbal blend with one cup of mugwort, ½ cup rose petals, ⅓ cup chamomile, ⅓ cup lavender, ⅓ cup catnip and two tablespoons mint. Blend all ingredients together and use two tablespoons per dream pillow.

Restful Sleep, the other popular blend, is for people who have trouble sleeping or are having nightmares. Blend ½ cup lavender, ½ cup mugwort, and ½ cup sweet hops. Put two tablespoons in each dream pillow.

Promote Your Herb Business

Most local newspapers provide a free "plug" for new businesses. Check with yours to see what they offer. Before you call, think about what makes your herb business unique or special, and mention that to the newspaper reporter or editor. They may like it enough to do a feature story! Another technique that works well is to offer something free – free classes, free herbal tea – and send out a simple press release announcing it.

Business cards and handouts. Always have these ready to give away. Make sure they're useful. One grower always puts a popular herbal recipe on the back of her business card, and says customers will never throw them away!

Classes. Many herb growers have found that classes are a great way to find new customers as well as bring in some extra income in the slow months. The most popular classes are: *Herbal Soapmaking, Making Herbal Cosmetics at Home, and Aromatherapy.*

Start your own product line. Herbal soaps and other body care products that you can easily produce at home are steady sellers and could be the start of your million-dollar success story. Sandy Maine started growing herbs, added herbal soaps, and grew her business to over a million dollars in annual sales. View her web site at: www.sunfeather.com.

Get creative with product names. One herb grower named one of her dream pillows *"Monster Chasing Pillow"*, tried it out on her kids – who loved it – and then added: *"Kid Tested, Mother Approved"* to the label. Sales doubled!

CHAPTER 10

Setting Goals

Goal setting is at the top of my "must-do" list for business success, including a plant-growing business. Setting goals helps you think about your future and close the gap between where you are now and where you want to be next year or even further into the future.

The key to goal setting success is writing your goals down on paper. Just the act of writing them down makes them seem real and make them part of your new reality. Get started by writing all the goals for your new business as if you were guaranteed to succeed no matter what.

Think about what you really want, no matter how impossible it may seem to you now. Take some time to dream big! Next, list your goals in order of importance and pick your most important goal. Then ask yourself "What one small step can I take to get me closer to that goal." Then do it today, no matter how small it may seem to you. Just getting started is what counts.

"A goal without a plan is just a wish."

Never forget - every goal, large or small, can be achieved by taking tiny steps every day toward that goal. Breaking your goal into smaller steps can build momentum and reduce the pressure of trying to deal with large goals.

Starting a new business is a large goal, and can seem overwhelming at first glance, but by breaking it down into small daily steps, it becomes much easier and not so overwhelming.

Action Steps

1. Write down what you really want.
2. Write down how you'll get there.
3. Write down your first step towards your most important goal.

"Find something you love to do, and you'll never have to work a day in your life."

GROUCHO MARX

Setting Realistic Goals

If you don't feel you can reach a goal because it seems overwhelming or you doubt your ability to achieve the goal, it's time to break it down to more manageable "mini-goals." Henry Ford once said *"Nothing is particularly hard if you break it down into small jobs."*

For example, if your goal of making $60,000 yearly in 2 years with your new business seems too big, break that goal into smaller goals. Set monthly goals, a 6-month goal, and a 1 year goal that are smaller and easier to achieve.

Deadlines

"A goal is a dream with a deadline."

It's important to set deadlines for your goals and the smaller steps to reaching the big goal. For example, say you'll add a new mini-greenhouse by October 30th. As you meet your deadlines, you'll build self-confidence and strengthen your belief that your goals are within reach.

Action Step:

Write down deadlines for all your goals - large and small.

"Most people underestimate what they can do in one year and underestimate what they can do in ten years."

BILL GATES

Most of us are too optimistic when setting goals and making plans. So it's not uncommon for things to take longer than expected. If that happens, don't quit or give up! Stick with your goal and realize that you WILL get there, even if it takes a while longer than you thought.

The 80/20 Rule

In working toward your goal, you'll find that 20% of your efforts will bring 80% of your progress towards that goal. This rule may not seem logical, but it has proven to hold true across a wide variety of situations and businesses.

So it's important that you find the things that will have the most impact and spend more of your time on them. Here's how to find your personal top 20%:

Make a list of all the things you can think of that could help you achieve your goal. Aim for at least 10 things, 20 is better.

Next, ask yourself, "If I could only do one thing on my list, which one will help me the most in reaching my goal?" Now go through the list again and identify the second item that will help you the most. If your list has 10 items, the top 2 gives you your 20%.

Daily Actions

When you work on your goal every day, you'll see progress and help make your goal a reality. By taking small steps every day, you'll feel like your goal is closer and it will empower you to push on.

We all have busy lives, so it's important to set aside enough time each day to work on your goals. Just do what is comfortable at the start, and pledge to stick to it. As you become more at ease with your new daily routine, you can spend more time on it.

*"You cannot change your destination overnight,
but you can change your direction overnight."*

JIM ROHN

If you think you don't have enough time in your day to start a new business, you need to identify the distractions in your life and avoid them or get them under control. Some examples: Turn off your technology alerts! When you need to focus on starting and growing your new business, turn off your email, phone, social media and chat.

Next, stop watching so much television, especially the news. The average person now spends several hours a day watching TV, and you can put that time towards growing a profitable business and a better life. Don't let these distractions control you!

*"Success is nothing more than a few simple
disciplines, practiced every day."*

JIM ROHN

Limiting Beliefs

Limiting beliefs can hold you back and create a false reality that can keep you from succeeding in your new business. The most common limiting belief when you're starting a new business is "It's too difficult" or "I'm not smart enough."

These limiting beliefs can cause you to put things off or quit at the least sign of failure or difficulty. Having these negative thoughts is normal, but never allow them to prevent you from moving forward.

When you have negative thoughts, give yourself permission to let them go. Replace these negative thoughts and limiting beliefs with more positive and empowering ones. Instead of "I can't do this," use "My new business will allow me to have a life I love."

Visualize Your Success

Imagination is one of the most powerful tools for improving your life and increasing your odds of business success. The more you visualize your goals, the more confident you'll become about your ability to reach those goals.

Take a few minutes every morning to visualize your goals and imagine how you will feel when you reach those goals. This will give you confidence and empower you to continue to take the steps necessary to reach your goals.

Action Steps

1. Focus on positive visualization every day that encourages action.

2. Remove negativity from your life and focus on the positive side. Your glass is half-full, not half-empty!

3. Every day, imagine your business is a huge success, and be confident it will be.

"For things to change, YOU have to change. For things to get better, YOU have to get better. For things to improve, YOU have to improve. When YOU grow, EVERYTHING in your life grows with you."

JIM ROHN

CHAPTER 11

Marketing Your New Plant Nursery Business

Without new customers, your nursery will never thrive and make a profit. Marketing is an essential part of starting and growing your new business, and this chapter will give you the tools to find all the customers you want, with very little expense.

Business owners today have far more marketing options available to them than just a few years ago. Now, because of the explosive growth of the internet as an advertising medium, many of the most effective marketing tools are free or close to it.

In additional to internet-based marketing, there are also dozens of traditional marketing methods available for any business owner that takes the time to use them. Almost all are free or almost free.

From flyers to publicity releases, smart small business owners have been using these proven methods to boost sales and profits for many years, but now, thanks to the internet, your marketing message can reach more people for less money than ever before.

Until recently, business owners had few options, and had to pay a high price for newspaper and yellow-page ads and printed mailers. Today, if you use a few simple internet-based marketing methods, the cost is close to zero.

Never forget the Golden Rule of marketing - treat your customers and prospects as you would want to be treated, and they will be loyal customers for life!

It's All About You

We see testimonials everywhere, from celebrity endorsements to local folks praising the peach cobbler at Andy's Diner. That's because they work, and better yet, unlike paid advertising, testimonials are free! If you're just getting started with your nursery business, free is good.

The Internet has given your customers the ability to spread the good news about your business to thousands of people overnight. If you learn how to use the web to encourage testimonials from happy clients, you'll be way ahead of most other businesses.

Another bonus from asking for testimonials is that unhappy clients will also respond, so you'll have an opportunity to correct whatever issue that made them unhappy.

It's important to encourage your customers to spread the word about your plant nursery because that can help you bring in more customers and sell more plants. Here are a few simple ways to do that:

At the end of every email or newsletter you send out, ask your customers for feedback. It doesn't have to be anything fancy, just a simple "How are we doing" or "We appreciate your feedback."

As you gather testimonials, post them on websites such as Citysearch.com or social networks that you use, such as Facebook, which provides "social proof" that can be even more powerful and far-reaching than a printed testimonial. I'll cover this in greater detail, including a list of several websites you can use at no cost just ahead.

When posting or printing a testimonial, provide as much information as possible - a picture, a first name and a city can dramatically increase the credibility. Be sure you have a customer's permission for anything you use in print or online.

Your customer's praise, in the form of a testimonial, is the best form of advertising money can't buy, so make it easy for your customers to help you succeed.

The Best Free Advertising

Satisfied customers are a small business "secret weapon," as they are usually repeat/regular customers and they tell their friends about your business, yet your out-of-pocket advertising cost is zero. Word-of-mouth can be your most effective advertising if you provide plants that are so good your customers return every year for more.

Always give your customers more than what they expect. Zappo's does it with free shipping and 110% customer service, bakers do it with the "baker's dozen" of an extra roll or pastry. Think about how you might surprise customers with an extra plant other unexpected bonus.

Networking - How to Do It Right

"You can have everything in life you want if you will just help other people get what they want."

ZIG ZIGLAR

Networking is one of the most effective ways to build your nursery business. It cost almost nothing - just your time. It's about building relationships with others with the goal of mutual benefit. It's more than passing out business cards. Networking is a two-way street, not just about trying to get something out of someone.

Networking is also about building trust. People always prefer to buy a product or service from someone they know, like and trust. Think about it. Would you rather buy plants from someone you don't know or visit a friend who also happens to sell plants?

Yet, if you're shy like me and so many others, just the thought of networking can be intimidating. When networking, remember you are building relationships, not make a sale. Here are a few proven tips to get you started:

1. Be genuine. Don't try to be someone else. If you're not a natural extrovert, that's perfectly okay.

2. Networking is about making friends. If you've ever made friends, you know how to network.

3. No one cares about you. All they care about is themselves. That's why you need to give something to other people you meet, whether they're potential customers or existing clients, without expecting them to do something in return.

4. When you give something to others, it creates an unspoken, often subconscious, need to return the favor. That's why networking works so well.

5. Be visible. Networking is a contact sport and the more people you contact and become visible to, the more you will build your business through networking.

7. When you're talking with someone, listen more than you speak. Give them your full attention and make them feel important by listening to them. When you do that, they will trust, like and respect you.

8. In your conversations with others, practice your ABCs (Always Be Curious). Ask what they do, ask about their family, what they do for fun.

9. Just do it - start a conversation with someone you haven't met yet and don't forget your ABCs.

Networking is an easy way to gain exposure for your nursery business in the community. Groups such as the Chamber of Commerce, Rotary and Kiwanis, and other business organizations can provide an opportunity to meet, greet, and become better known. Besides groups, spread the word among related businesses, such as garden clubs or other plant nurseries.

A Smile is Still the Best Free Advertising

A simple smile is rarely mentioned in advertising textbooks or classes, but it is one of the most important marketing tools we all possess. A smile forms a powerful human bond and shows you regard a person as a human being, not just another customer or business prospect.

A smile makes a person feel good, and perhaps even feel you are a friend. As you know, folks like to buy from friends. Ask yourself how you felt the last time someone smiled at you. How did it make you feel? I thought so. Remember, smiles are free, requiring only a small amount of energy. Don't forget that a smile works when you're chatting on the phone, as the person on the other end can actually feel the smile.

Business success is all about paying attention to the little details, like a genuine smile. Share yours with every customer and prospect you meet and let it work its magic for you.

Customer Service

Marketing pros rank customer service right up there in the top three success factors for small business. In these competitive times, running a customer- focused business can make the difference between success and failure. Like most of the ideas in this chapter, customer service costs almost nothing out- of-pocket.

Customer service should be based on the needs of your customers. If you pay attention to their needs and wants, your business will thrive. Your success depends on repeat customers. Never forget that a customer's value is not what they are spending today, but what they might spend over a lifetime as your loyal customer.

Listen to your customers. A happy customer will tell five friends about your business, while an unhappy one may tell ten! One way to ensure there are no unhappy customers is to ask for feedback regularly.

Get a rubber stamp that reads: "How Am I Doing?" and stamp it on every bill you send out, so clients can give you feedback. You can do that on your website too.

Why You Should Love Complaints

Complaints can be a powerful marketing tool if you encourage them and handle them well. Once a month, check in with your regular customers to ask them how you're doing. Ask if they are happy with your plants and services. Could it be better? Any services they would like to see added?

When you do this, you might get complaints—some mild and some not so mild. That's okay. You want customers to complain, and here's why:

- Unhappy customers tell others about you. That won't happen if you listen and correct any problems.

- If your customers don't complain, you'll never know of any problems and won't be able to fix them.

- If one customer is having a problem, others could too. Even if customers don't complain, when they are unhappy with your plants and service, they are likely to switch to your competition.

Here's a simple four-step method for turning complaints into happy customers:

1. **Say "I'm sorry."** These two powerful words can calm an angry customer and let them know you accept responsibility.

2. **Find a solution.** First, let them talk to be sure you understand the reason they have a complaint. After you are sure you "get it", do what is necessary to resolve the problem quickly.

3. **Thank your customer.** Let them know you appreciate bringing the problem to your attention and ask them to let you know the next time there is a problem.

4. **Follow up.** After you have solved the problem that prompted the customer's complaint, follow up in person, if possible, to let them know what you did for them, and ask if that is acceptable for them.

Traditional Marketing

For many, finding customers is the most challenging part of starting a new business. Don't worry. There are many free and low-cost ways to spread the word about your new nursery business, and we'll explore a few of the best here.

Newspaper ads. Most local newspapers have a "service directory" or something similar, where you can run a regular classified or display ad for your business at a reduced rate. It's best to keep the ad small but repeat it regularly once a week during the spring and summer is about right. Repetition is the secret to successful advertising. After a few months, readers will remember your ad and look for it when they need plants.

Free classifieds. You can place a free classified ad at www. Craigslist.org. Use the region and city-specific sections, so you can get the word out to just those in your target area.

Business cards. Business cards are an essential sales tool to pass out to everyone who is a prospect for your plants and to those who may refer customers to you.

For the best selection and pricing on business cards, try www. Vistaprint.com. Vistaprint has hundreds of "stock" designs to choose from Use both sides of the card. On the front, include your business name & slogan, address and phone, e-mail address and a website address. On the back, list the plants you offer, and if you have room, "don't see a plant - call and ask."

Custom note pads. One of the best ways to keep your name in front of repeat customers like landscapers every day is custom note pads. Other forms of marketing materials may get tossed, but people always appreciate and use note pads or scratch pads.

Notepads give you what marketers call "top of the mind awareness." When someone thinks of landscaping plants, they also think of you. Every time they need to make a note, it reminds them of your business. Your customers and prospects will have your name in front of them daily, and when a note gets passed on to someone else, your name is in front of them as well.

In addition, instead of having to remember your contact information when they need a delivery or pickup, it's right there in front of them! Don't skip this powerful marketing tool—pass out three or four pads to each customer and prospect. Here are sources for affordable notepads:

www.notepadsinc.com

www.customprintednotepads.com

www.marcopromotionalproducts.com

Magnetic signs. You'll be amazed at how much business you will get from customers who saw the sign on your vehicle. Unlike a yellow page ad, there is just a one-time cost of around $60. Vistaprint can also create a custom magnetic sign for you, as can www.magneticsigns.com. If you're looking for a vinyl sign for the rear of your vehicle, try www.fastsigns.com.

Make Money with Reminders

Your existing customers are like money in the bank. They know you; they trust you and are far more likely to purchase from you than someone who is not yet a customer. One of the easiest ways for a business to make money is to contact past customers with a special offer.

For example, send out an e-mail coupon to your client and prospect mailing list every month. The coupon could be for specials, like a 10% discount for a new customer, or a non- specific offer, like 20% off when a customer spends $300.

Internet Marketing

How to Set Up Your Own Nursery Business Website

A simple website is the best way to advertise your plant nursery. A website is the 21st century version of traditional Yellow Pages advertising, because most prospects expect to find your business, or any other services and products, on the Internet.

If you think putting up a website is expensive, think again. The cost of hosting a website has dropped over the last few years, so today you can get high quality hosting for under $10 a month, with all the bells and whistles that used to be expensive add-ons now included free with hosting.

Today, a website is an essential marketing tool for any business, and even more so for a plant nursery. A basic, no-frills website can help you find new customers and stay in touch with existing customers.

If you're new to building a website, make a list of what you want to accomplish before building your site. For example, do you want to make it easy for new prospects to learn more about your business before they contact you? You'd be surprised at how many prospects do not know what types of plants you specialize in so have a page listing your plants. An "About" page can be warm and fuzzy, with a picture or two of your family, your dog, or local scenic attractions.

Most basic nursery business websites include an FAQ page that contains all the frequently asked questions (FAQs) and answers about your nursery, a contact page with both phone and email contact information, a page listing the plants you offer, and, after you have them and testimonials from satisfied customers. It's helpful to visit other plant nursery websites to see what others are doing.

If you are like most new business startups, your advertising/ marketing budget is tiny. Why not harness the power of the Internet to build your business, without spending a lot of money, by signing up for website hosting with a company that offers not only affordable hosting services but also free help to create your website?

You may have heard about hosting companies that offer free hosting, but here's why you should only consider paid hosting for your small business website:

1. You can use and control, your own personal or business domain name, such as "rosesunlimited.com". When you have registered your domain name, you own the name which can help your search engine visibility when prospects search for a plant nursery or specific variety of plant.

2. Paid web hosting is very affordable, and you will get better tools and resources to help you create and maintain your website.

3. No ads. Free hosting companies may place ads on your website. That's how they make money, even though your website hosting is technically "free."

I'm a big fan of WordPress to build a website. Although it started as a blogging program, WordPress has now become a capable, yet user- friendly site builder that can be customized to meet the needs of almost any business.

With thousands of free themes and free help from a huge online forum of users, it may be the best way to build an affordable website. In addition, there are thousands of "widgets" and "plugins" that can be added to your website to provide additional features like videos, shopping carts, or customer surveys.

Even if you're not a tech-savvy person, setting up, maintaining and adding to your site is easy enough for most users to do themselves, especially with the detailed free videos detailing how to do just about anything with WordPress.

I use SiteGround for my website hosting, because it's so easy to use, with a free domain name, 1-click automatic WordPress installation, free email accounts, and great customer service by phone, chat or email 24/7. I highly recommend SiteGround for your first website.

Get started by visiting the SiteGround.com website and clicking the "Get Started" button, then choose the more affordable "Start-Up" plan. Next, register your new domain name, which should match your business name as closely as possible.

Take some time with this, as you want a domain name that makes it easy for prospects and customers to find you when searching the internet. Here are a few tips to help you do it right.

- The shorter your domain name, the easier it will be to remember. Aim for two or three words where possible.
- The fewer the characters, the better. The average number of characters in the top websites is just 9. Think Amazon.com
- Pick a name that gives visitors some idea of what they will find at your website or what your business does.
- Don't use numbers in your domain name because they are easy to forget.
- Say the name of your new domain name out loud. The best are easy to say and stick with you. For example, Google, Facebook and YouTube.
- Make a list of domain names you are considering and ask friends and family what they think.
- Having trouble coming up with good names? Search for websites that are in the same business as you. Doing this will also help you rule out names that are already taken.
- Make sure your choice of names is not in use or trademarked by someone else.
- Pick a ".com" extension for your domain name, as it is more trusted by the public than lesser-used extensions like ".biz" or ".info"

For more domain name ideas, search for "domain name generator" online. One of the free services that pops up can generate names you may never have thought of.

To build your website, you can choose WordPress or Weebly. Both website builders are provided free at SiteGround. Weebly is the best choice for first-time users, as its drag-and-drop interface is very easy to use.

Once you've chosen your domain name, you'll be asked to choose your plan. My advice is to stick to a basic plan, as it's affordable and provides everything you need to start up and claim your slice of the Internet.

On their website, and on YouTube, SiteGround.com has dozens of free videos explaining how to set up and manage your website. Just visit YouTube.com and type "SiteGround" in the search bar. If you would rather have professional help to set up your website, visit Fiverr.com and search for "build a website."

Congratulations! You're almost there with your new website. Take the time to watch the videos and add the pages you need to help prospects and customers find your business online. Be sure to add your website address to your other printed materials, such as business cards, flyers, and brochures so your customers can easily find you online.

If you get stuck, or have a question, or need a new theme or plugin, help is just a click away at wordpress.org. WordPress has a very active member forum, where you can get your questions answered at no cost. Just visit the site and click on "support" in the top menu bar. Also, SiteGround has an excellent tech support team, which you can access at their website.

Let Google Help Your Customers Find You

 If your business depends on local customers, you'll enjoy a free listing in Google Places. Today, most of your customers are using internet search engines to find local services and businesses instead of the traditional Yellow Pages. So it makes sense to take advantage of these free listings offered by online directories for businesses. The most popular, and currently the largest, of all is Google Places.

You can start by visiting http://places.google.com and clicking on the 'get started now' button under 'Get your business found on Google.' After signing in, or signing up, at no cost, you'll be able to list your business. You can include photos or add photos or a map.

Getting a basic listing is simple, but there are a few ways to help your business appear near the top of the listings if you have any local competitors listed.

First, remember Google values good content, so be sure you fill out your business profile with quality information. Follow their directions for completing the listing to the letter and don't leave any blank spaces.

Next, encourage your customers to leave feedback and positive reviews on any websites related to your business, such as local directories published by groups like the Chamber of Commerce. You can also ask customers to leave reviews or testimonials on your own website but be sure they are legitimate and genuine.

Last, if you don't have one yet, your business needs a website, ideally with its own domain name. Having a website will give your business, however small it is, a giant boost in the Google rankings.

As more and more businesses sign up for Google Places, those who have a website will have a better shot at a listing near the top. Almost any web hosting service, such as SiteGround, mentioned earlier, can help you get a domain name and set up a Wordpress site, which ranks well with Google, as Wordpress is easy to index.

Besides Google Places, other major online 'local' directories worth exploring are:

http://bing.com/local

http://listings.local.yahoo.com

http://yelp.com

http://linkedin.com

http://citysearch.com

http://listings.mapquest.com

http://advertise.local.com

http://angieslist.com

Local S.E.O.

Since your new plant nursery will depend on local customers, you must use location-based keywords, such as "courier your town." The reason local SEO (Search Engine Optimization) is so important for your business is because almost half of all Google searches are searching for a local business. Plus, the fastest growing search term on Google is "near me" as in "Italian restaurant near me."

Since Google and other search engines can easily determine your approximate location, this enables them to deliver the results you are searching for with high accuracy.

To make it even easier for you to find what you're looking for, Google provides a "Map Pack," a set of 3 high ranking local businesses, complete with a map of their locations from Google maps. Underneath the Map Pack, you'll find the rest of the results for your search.

How to find the best keywords for local S.E.O.

Do a Google search for words and phrases that relate to your business, one at a time, and make a list of them. For example, "plant nursery near me," "landscaping trees my town," "plant nursery near me," "flowers my town."

When you enter your search term, you'll see a list of additional search terms. Take a close look at those to see if any are suitable for your business. Save your list of search terms to use when setting up your "Google My Business" profile.

How to Set Up Your "Google My Business" Profile

Google My Business (www.google.com/business) is the number one factor Google uses to rank your business in local searches. When setting up your profile, be sure to include your full business name, address, and phone number (NAP). Google uses this information to ensure that your business is legitimate. Also, the NAP on your website should be an exact match for your Google My Business listing.

If it's not a match, Google may rank your business lower in local searches. Even spelling counts here - if your business address is 123 Lincoln Avenue, makes sure it's "Avenue" and not "Ave." so the Google search engine doesn't get confused.

When filling out your profile on GMB, choose a broad category that best describes your business - "landscaping plants" for example. You can then choose sub-categories, such as "landscaping plants" or "potted herbs." Also fill out the "services" tab in your profile that describes what your business does.

Google Reviews

Reviews are another major ranking factor in the Google ranking system. You may have noticed that business with many reviews, especially positive reviews, always ranks higher than those with no reviews. So you'll want to get as many positive reviews as you can as soon as you can.

When you get a review, good, bad or lukewarm, reply to it inside the Google My Business dashboard. That shows you care and is also a factor in Google rankings. It doesn't have to be a long reply to be effective. For example, "Thanks for the 5-star review. We really appreciate your business," or "We're sorry your shrub lost so many leaves and promise we'll do better next time. Thanks for the feedback."

How to Get More Google Reviews

Keep in mind that most customers won't bother to leave a review, even if they love your service, unless asked. It's easy to do. In fact, Google makes it easy for both you and your customers.

Go to your GMB account dashboard and locate the "get more reviews" card. There, you can get a link to your review page that you can copy and paste into an email to send to your customers.

Apply all these simple SEO tips, and soon your new business will show up on page 1 of Google search results. All without having to spend any money. Don't put this off any longer than necessary, as it's one of the best "free lunches" you'll ever receive!

Social Media Marketing

Facebook - Facebook is the largest social media network in the world, with over 2 billion active users. Because of its size and the large number of users, Facebook is the best social media to get your new business shared and discovered by both new prospects and your current customers. That's why it is often called "the largest word-of-mouth marketing resource on the planet."

Facebook can also be the biggest time waster if you let, as it's easy to linger there for hours. But you have a business to build and grow, so let's focus on doing just that, with some help from Facebook, in less than 15 minutes a day.

First rule - don't waste your money on Facebook ads. No one visits Facebook to look for services or products. They visit to see what their friends are doing. With that in mind, here's how to get started without spending a dime.

It's important to note that you must create a Facebook page, not a personal profile, also called a Personal Timeline. They do not permit personal profiles for commercial use, so if you are already a Facebook user, you must create a separate page for your nursery business.

You can create a Facebook Page by searching "create a page" in the searcher at the top of the page, or by clicking the "create a page" button at the top of any Facebook page.

Before you create your new Facebook page, spend some time thinking about the page name you will use. Ideally, it should be short, easy to remember, promise a benefit, and describe your business. A good example would be (if your nursery business is in Tampa) @tampaplantnursery.

In the "About" section of your new Facebook Page, include as much information about your business as possible, so current clients and prospects can find all your important information in one page.

You can also optimize your page by choosing one of the pre-made templates. You'll find the templates under: Settings>Edit Page. Next, create an eye-catching cover photo for your Facebook page. Look at other plant nursery businesses, both on Facebook and by doing a web search for "plant nursery business" or "landscaping plants" to see what others have done.

Ideally, your cover photo should communicate what your courier business is all about, so take the time to do it right. The easiest way to get a good cover photo designed is to hire a designer at Fiverr.com. It will cost you around $5 to $15, but it's money well spent.

Just enter "design Facebook cover" in the Fiverr.com search bar to locate dozens of capable designers. Be sure to mention that you want the image size to be 820 X 312 pixels per Facebook guidelines.

When you've uploaded your new cover photo, click it to add a text description. Describe your business in a positive way and, if possible, encourage viewers to click on the cover photo to get more "likes."

You'll also want to add a Facebook profile photo in a 180 x 180 pixel size. Remember, this profile photo appears in a follower's news feeds, in comment replies, and all over Facebook, so use a great photo. (Don't forget to smile!)

Once you've set up your Facebook page, stay active with regular posts. Most pros find 3X a week works well yet doesn't require a lot of time. Don't forget to post about special experiences you've had, such as landscaping projects that others might enjoy. Share the story and a picture or two of you and your customers in a post.

Is a Facebook Page Better Than a Web Site?

Yes, and no. You can set up a Facebook page in about an hour and it's free. That page allows you to stay in touch with clients and prospects and build relationships. If a Facebook page is not working for you delete it or ignore it. Keeping your Facebook page up to date with your current information, such as a current plan list and prices, is quick and easy.

But - you are not in control. Facebook is in control and can change or restrict what you can do there overnight. In addition, anyone can post negative comments or complaints on your page if they wish.

If you create a website, you're in control. You own it. You get to decide what it looks like and what it contains. You can have hundreds of pages/ posts or just a simple one-pager.

Consumers today expect a business to have a website. They trust a business more when they see a "real" website. Also, having your own website allows you to post all your plant information at the site, like the plants you grow, monthly specials, testimonials and more.

My choice would be to have both a Facebook page and a website. You have the best of both worlds - and you don't have to say "follow me on Facebook."

Twitter - Twitter can be a powerful social media tool for your plant nursery that can help you educate customers about your plants and services, reach new prospects for your business and connect you to other Twitter users with similar interests.

Here are just two of the many ways Twitter can help your business:

1. Drive traffic to your website. Unlike other social media, you can reuse content from your website or other original material repeatedly. Your tweets can include your website URL, text, images, even a video.

2. Google indexes your twitter bio and tweets, which helps you get found by search engines. Make sure your bio contains the keywords you want Google to find and index, such as your business name and what your business does. Be sure to tweet regularly so you increase the odds of ranking higher in Google Search.

3. Last, use hashtags (#) to get more attention for your tweets, show your support and help people who don't know you to follow you. To learn what topics are hot or trending up right now, check Twitter Trends or hashtagify.me.

It's free and easy to make an account - just visit twitter.com, enter your name, phone and email address and create a password for your new account. After you've signed up, you can add more information for your account.

Next it's time to pick your Twitter "handle," which is the same as a username. The best handle is your business name, if it is available. You can check all the social networks for name availability at knowem.com.

If your handle/name is not available, you can add HQ to your company name, add a "get" in front of your name, or add your location, such as your town's name, to your handle.

Whatever handle you choose, make sure it is as short as possible, because you only have 280 characters to use, and they count your username in that 280 words when someone responds to your messages.

LinkedIn - LinkedIn is a place for companies and individuals to connect on a professional, not personal, level. Unlike other social media sites, folks who join LinkedIn are not joining for enjoyment and fun but to access new business opportunities and connections.

As the owner of a small business, you can use LinkedIn to connect to other nursery businesses, promote your own business and build relationships with other professionals that have common interests.

Getting started is no more difficult than at other social networks. You start by creating your own personal account and profile. A LinkedIn profile is much more professional. You won't find funny cat videos or cute baby photos.

Keep that in mind when creating your profile. In your profile be sure to include your best work-related qualities so others will see the advantages of working with you.

Although you can upgrade to several higher levels of paid subscriptions, the basic account should be fine for almost all nursery businesses. Your basic profile can include a summary of yourself, contact information, links to your blog or website or other social media pages, like Facebook, and what you're doing now professionally.

Be sure to add a high-quality photo of yourself, as people are much more at ease connecting to someone with a photo.

Once you've completed your personal profile and published it, you can:

1. Look for connections - people you know or would like to know.
2. Join a group of other users who share common interests.
3. Have an online "business card" where potential clients can learn about and connect with you.
4. Boost your online reputation as a plant professional.

There are hundreds of other social media sites, as you may have noticed when you visited knowem.com. but most are useful only for entertainment, not helping you grow your nursery business. These three, Facebook, Twitter and LinkedIn will help you stay connected, expand your network, and increase your profits.

Email Marketing

Stay in Touch with a Free Newsletter

One of the best and least expensive ways to stay in touch with your clients and potential clients is by sending them an e-mail newsletter. By using an email, the big expenses of a traditional newsletter, printing and postage, are eliminated. Your newsletter should do two things:

1. Pass along useful information your customers are happy to read, even forward to their friends.
2. Increase your profits by either helping sell more of your services or attract more prospects who will buy from you.

The easiest way to make sure your newsletter accomplishes those two goals is to just ask your customers and prospects what they want before you send out the first issue and keep asking them what they want in the newsletter. How often should a newsletter be sent to customers? Most experts say it's not how often that matters, but the quality of the content. Some prefer a frequent schedule, such as every two weeks or once a month, while others may only do a quarterly newsletter. If you have built a list of loyal customers, they don't really care how often they receive an issue.

Be sure to ask a favor at the end of each newsletter: *"If you've enjoyed this newsletter, please forward it to your friends."* Doing so will grow your subscriber list and your profits over time.

When your e-mail list has grown beyond a few subscribers, it's time to get some professional help. My favorites are www.MailChimp.com and www.mailerlite.com

At Mail Chimp, for free, you'll have access to professionally designed message templates and sign-up forms, and up to 2,000 customers or 12,000 emails a month and compliance with all anti-spam regulations. You'll love the free service, plus the freedom from tedious mailing list maintenance. Another excellent provider with free service for up to 1,000 subscribers is mailerlite.com.

Ten Tips for a Successful E-Mail Newsletter

According to the e-mail pros, a well-done e-mail newsletter can produce $40 in profits for every dollar you spend. That's a powerful incentive to spend the time on staying in touch with your customers and prospects with e-mails. Here are ten tips that will help you make more money and build customer loyalty with your own e-mail newsletter.

1. Current content. Be sure to date each newsletter issue when you send it out so readers will know the content is current.

2. You don't have to be a writer to produce an e-mail newsletter that gets results. Just write as you speak and focus on the topic you want to communicate with your clients.

3. Your newsletter need not look professional to succeed. Just a simple text message will work just fine. That said, most of the professional e-mail list management services, like www.MailerLite.com.com and www.MailChimp.com offer free HTML templates that can dress up your message.

4. The best ideas for content in your e-mail newsletter will come from your readers. Ask them often about what they would like to see covered in future issues.

5. Keep your newsletter short. If you have several ideas to share, break them up into individual newsletter issues, or include an excerpt, with a link to the full text at your web site or blog.

6. Try not to go too long between issues – two weeks to a month is a reasonable interval to aim for.

7. The cyber-gremlins will always try to mess with your e-mails, so get used to it. E-mails get lost, trapped in reader's spam filters, or just plain disappear. Subscribers will forget they subscribed and accuse you of spamming them or click the spam button instead of unsubscribing. Just view it all as a part of your learning curve and stay calm. Using one of the services mentioned in #3 can help minimize problems, and the cost is reasonable. In fact, as I write this, Mail Chimp and Mailer Lite offer a free service if you have a small (under 2,000 subscribers) list.

8. Keep your sales pitches under control. While folks expect you to sell them something, they get upset if it occurs with every newsletter issue. Experts say a ratio of 80 percent informational content to 20 percent sales information is about right.

9. Stay on topic. Your readers gave you their e-mail address so they could learn more about topics related to getting packages from point A to point B affordably, and other related topics. Stay away from personal topics, as some will enjoy learning about your personal life, but an equal amount will not care, and be inclined to hit the spam button or unsubscribe.

10. Post your newsletters on your website so readers can find them at a later date. In addition, the search engines will spot and index them, and help steer new prospects to your site.

CHAPTER 12

Business Basics

How To License Your New Nursery Business

First - pick a name! This is an important step, so be sure to take the time to follow these suggestions and do it right! Start by making a list of several possible business names that best describe your new business. Pick a name that suggests what your company is all about, as that name is the first impression a prospective customer will have.

Adding the name of your town tells prospects your service area, as well as making it easier for the search engines, such as Google, to find your website when you set it up. That's super important, as most prospects locate a local business using web search.

Be sure to choose a name that is easy to spell and remember. Before you make your final selection, get feedback from family or friends. Do they like it? Could it be improved?

After you've chosen a name, verify that you can use the name. Start by checking to see if the name can be registered as a domain name, as you'll need a website containing your company name to help customers and prospects contact you online and learn more about your services. If a domain name is unavailable, try adding the name of your town or area to it and check availability again.

Next, check with your county clerk's office to see if your proposed business name is being used by anyone else. If you plan to use an LLC legal structure, check with your state's corporate filing office or Secretary of State.

Last, do a federal trademark search (free at USPTO.gov) of the name you've chosen to ensure no one else is using the name, or if your use of the name would confuse someone.

Now that you've made sure your chosen business name is available and you can get a matching domain name, it's time to register the name. In most cases, this is handled by your local county clerk's office.

In most areas, you'll need two different types of licensing for your plant nursery. First, you'll need a business license, usually supplied by your state, city or county. This license will allow you to buy plants and supplies at wholesale prices from suppliers.

A federal tax identification number, issued by the Internal Revenue Service, (www.irs.gov) is usually required before you can get your business license. Start with the IRS, as you'll need the "Employer Identification Number," or EIN, when you apply for other licenses, permits, and a bank account. Visit the IRS website at www.irs.gov and enter "Form SS4" in the search window.

Next, you can print the application form or apply online. Applying online is much faster, and you can get your EIN when you've finished filling out the form!

Second, you may need a special license or permit to operate a plant nursery, which is usually issued by your state department of agriculture. The fee for a nursery license is often based on the size of the nursery and covers the cost of an annual inspection by an agricultural inspector.

Most states also require a resale license if there is a state sales tax. This requires you to collect sales tax on retail sales and get an exemption certificate from any purchasers who plan to resell your plants. It also allows you to buy your supplies that are resold, such as pots, without paying sales tax.

Taxes and Accounting

There are three types of taxes you'll be responsible for as a business owner, employment taxes, income tax and self-employment tax. If you do not have employees, you rarely have to pay employment taxes, but just a self-employment tax.

It's a good idea to visit a tax pro, such as an accountant, to learn just what taxes are due for the legal type of business you plan to start, such as an LLC. They can also advise you what information they will require to help you at tax time, such as a profit-and-loss statement.

To keep accounting costs low, do as much as possible yourself. Today, most accounting software for small businesses has gone online and is called "cloud" software, as it is web- hosted rather than from a program installed on your computer. This allows the software company to update programs regularly to reflect changes in tax laws and other regulations.

A nursery does not need a high-powered, expensive accounting system, but something that is simple enough to be easy to understand and use. It should also be capable of generating invoices for your clients and reports needed by your accountant or tax professional.

As I write this, there are over a dozen capable accounting software programs suitable for your small business. They all have the basic capabilities covered, so it's up to you to choose the best fit for you. Here are my current favorites:

Fresh Books. This cloud-based accounting program is considered one of the best invoicing solutions available, which is important if you have landscapers to bill regularly. You can also add auto-billing and automatic payment reminders and thank-you notes!

Like most, they offer a free trial period so new users can see if they like the program before spending any money. They base their pricing on the number of clients you bill.

Because it is web-based, there are no downloads or installations, and it is compatible with all operating systems as long as you have internet access.

Fresh Books is very easy to use, a big plus for a non-accountant like me (and you?) The setup is simple and quick, and the interface is easy to figure out and logical. Help is available online and by phone.

GoDaddy Bookkeeping. This software, formerly called Outright, is more user-friendly than most accounting programs. It's more of a bookkeeping program aimed at small businesses that just need to account for income, expenses and taxes.

The company was started by two guys who worked at Intuit, the parent company of Quickbooks, to offer a simpler solution for small business owners who didn't know much about accounting but needed to have accurate data for their taxes.

This software is also cloud-based, so there are no downloads, and you can access your account anywhere you have an internet connection, even on your iPad or smartphone. There is a free plan if you just need to track income and expenses, and a paid version which is affordable–currently about $120 per year.

Like all the other cloud accounting programs, you can link your accounts, such as bank accounts, credit cards, Paypal and other payment processing accounts. Then it automatically downloads the information daily and it can create and send invoices to customers.

Unlike most of the other online programs, there is no extra charge for additional customers. Whether you have two or two hundred, the cost is the same. To learn more, visit: https://www.GoDaddy.com/email/online- bookkeeping

Quickbooks Online. Everyone has heard of Quicken, which has been available since the mid-80s, followed by Quickbooks. It is the Big Dog of accounting software and is used by thousands of companies.

Quickbooks Online has a 3-tier pricing plan and a 30-day free trial. The basic "Simple Start" plan includes invoicing and estimates and all the normal accounting features. The "Essentials" plan adds an accounts payable function to track and pay bills. The "Plus" plan allows subscribers to track inventory and generate 1099 forms.

The software is web-hosted, so no downloads or installation is required, and is compatible with Windows and Mac OS X operating systems. Setup is easy and quick and includes several how-to videos. There are a huge number of features available to users, but the less-used ones are kept in the background for regular users.

When you send an invoice to your customers in FreshBooks, GoDaddy bookkeeping and Quicken, your customers can pay instantly by credit card, thanks to built-in payment processing. This means you'll get paid faster, and they don't have to hunt for a stamp and write a check. It's a win-win for both you and your customers.

Another advantage of using accounting/bookkeeping software is that you can set up the billing cycle so you receive a "red flag" reminder when the invoice is unpaid past a certain number of days.

The billing cycle used by most businesses is 30 days, so make it clear to your customers that there is a late fee for past due payments. Most businesses charge a percentage of the unpaid balance, such as 2% per month. If the bill is unpaid 10 days after the due date, the late fee applies.

Tax tip: Don't forget to keep track of your business-related mileage, as it is deductible at tax time. The current rate is around 58 cents per mile. To keep track of those business miles to take full advantage of the IRS deduction, you need to keep accurate records.

Fortunately, there are many apps that work on your smartphone that can track your miles so you don't waste time or forget to record trips. Here are a few of the best free apps to do that. Just visit the Apple store or Google Play to download them.

Easy Logbook. This is one of the simplest mileage tracking apps to use. All you do is hit the start button at the beginning of a trip and the stop button at the end, then label the trip. Then enter a trip description and you're done.

Everlance. Has great features for tracking business travel and is also designed to reduce the battery drawdown. You can even add receipts for gas and other travel-related expenses.

Mileguru. A simple yet complete app for tracking mileage and other deductible expenses. When you're ready, just send a report via PDF.

TrackMyDrive. This automatic mileage tracking app runs in the background on your phone and detects all your drives, then let's you store the information in the cloud. Also generates IRS tax reports.

Like most mileage tracking apps, the first few trips are free, then you need to upgrade. But this app is currently less than $10 per year, so it's quite affordable.

Show Me the Money - Getting Paid

When you send an invoice to your customers with your accounting software, your customers can pay instantly by credit card, thanks to built-in payment processing. This makes it much easier for them to pay their bill. This means you'll get paid faster, and they don't have to hunt for a stamp and write a check. It's a win-win for both you and your customers.

If you want a separate payment processing option, Square, the payment processing company whose terminals seem to be at the checkout counter of every restaurant, offers a virtual terminal, so you can take remote payments from your customers. Their "card on file" feature allows you to charge repeat customers on a regular basis at no extra cost.

I've used PayPal for many years and found them to be great to work with. Big advantage - almost everyone (over 250 million and growing) has a PayPal account. Your customers don't even need a PayPal account to pay you. It's amazingly easy to set up and get started in a day or so, and the rates are very competitive. Another advantage is that the PayPal system syncs with almost all shopping carts and accounting software.

In many parts of the world, mobile payment apps on a smartphone are becoming the default payment method of choice. In China, for example, cash is becoming obsolete, as everyone has WeChat on their smartphone, and in India, the WhatsApp is the payment method of choice. Cash, checks and credit cards are on the way out.

This is happening in the U.S. as well, with dozens of payment options such as Venmo, Apple Pay, Google Pay and Zelle. Venmo, which is owned by PayPal is the leader now, with an app that makes sending and receiving cash almost effortless. If a customer asks if you use Venmo or Apple Pay and you are not set up, the app is just a free download away at the iTunes store.

Finding Affordable Business Insurance

Business insurance provides financial protection and peace of mind for you and your new small business. Yet, over half of all home-based small businesses lack insurance coverage according to the Independent Insurance Agents and Brokers of America. One common reason is confusion over what is and isn't covered by homeowner's policies, renter's policies and vehicle policies.

If you have a small home-based business, as most startups do, you're in good company. After all, Amazon, Apple, Disney, Google, Harley Davidson and Microsoft, to name just a few well-known examples, were started in garages!

But no matter how small your new business is, you definitely need business insurance. You can choose from these three basic types of small business insurance:

1. A rider or endorsement to your homeowner's or renter's policy. Depending on your insurance company, you can get an add-on rider that will expand your insurance coverage to include your business. The cost is usually reasonable.

2. An in-home business policy covers a wide range of events, such as business equipment loss, injury and theft. You must talk to a local insurance agent or broker, as each state has its own rules about required coverage for these policies.

3. Business owner's policy. This comprehensive policy typically includes damage or loss to equipment, liability

coverage if a customer is injured, professional liability coverage, loss of business income and often includes coverage when you are driving a personal vehicle for business purposes.

The business owner's policy should provide a basic safety net for most small businesses. In most states you can get liability coverage extensions tailored to your specific business.

Other coverages - It may be necessary to have a business auto policy that covers any vehicles used for business purposes. Just like a personal vehicle policy, it typically covers both liability and physical damage coverage.

If your business has employees, you'll also need worker's compensation insurance, which is available through insurance companies in most states, and through a state insurance fund in Ohio, Washington, Wyoming and North Dakota.

If your state allows coverage by private insurance companies, shop around to find an insurer that has competitive rates and the specific coverage for your type of business.

When possible, use an insurance broker in your area who can get quotes from multiple insurance companies. Insurance brokers can also advise you on which companies have the best reputation for quick and fair claims handling.

Looking Good with A Logo

Having a logo is one of the most important new business requirements that can make your plant nursery memorable and show customers you're serious about your business. A logo can be simple, like the Target Stores bullseye, or more elaborate.

A well-done logo can help you market your nursery more effectively, displaying it on business cards, brochures, flyers, your website, and other marketing materials. People remember images more than printed words or talk. Your eye-catching logo can put that image in their mind so they associate the image with you and your business.

Here are a few points to remember about planning your logo:

A logo should be timeless, so you can use it for your business for decades. A logo should be simple and easy to understand and not confuse people.

Never, ever copy or design a logo similar to another, as it is an invitation to a lawsuit, and just plain lazy and unethical.

Will the logo still make sense as your business expands, adds services and grows?

Is the logo easy to see or read in all sizes, from a magnetic sign on your car to a thumbnail image on your business card?

Today, thanks to the many internet-based sources for logos, you can get a basic logo for just a few dollars. If you're on a very lean budget, visit Fiverr.com and search the site for "logo design."

You can spend as little as $5 at Fiverr, but my suggestion is to get a basic logo from two or three designers there and pick the one you like the best. (Give each one the same instructions about the look and color you want.) You can also have them take the finished logo you pick and make it into a "banner" or "header" for the top of your website.

At Fiverr.com, just enter "logo design" in the search bar to get started. You'll find hundreds to choose from, so I recommend using a "level one" or "level two" seller/designer who has at least 100 five-star reviews. That will narrow the field down and make it easier to find the best ones.

Explain to each logo designer what you want, such as text only, text and images, and the colors you prefer. When you have the 3 finished logo designs, pick your favorite, and add any extras from that designer you may want, like a header for your website using the new logo.

CHAPTER 13

Time to Grow – Adding New Employees

Whether you plan to hire new employees now or in the future, it's important to do it right. Because of the complexities of today's labor laws, federal and state regulations and record- keeping involved, you need to know of these requirements before you even place your first help wanted ad.

Hiring the best people for your nursery business will free you to focus on the "big picture" that will help you grow your business, give you a backup person who can take over when you are sick or on vacation and increase your profits when you add more plants or new customers.

After you have hired and trained your new employee, you will also gain precious time to keep learning more about your nursery business with workshops and seminars. You'll also gain the time to build your network which will help your business to grow.

As your business grows, you will gain new customers, but without help, you may have to turn away those new customers because you're already over-extended and over-worked! That's not good. In addition, with good help, you will serve your existing customers better.

When is it time to hire employees?

1. Do you feel you just can't ever take a day off? Without employees, you can forget vacations or sick days. Just one employee can give you the personal time you need and deserve.

2. Are you turning down new customers? When you have to say "no" to new customers or work longer hours just to keep up, it's time to get the help that will allow you to expand your business and become more profitable.

3. Are your customers unhappy? When your customers complain about poor service, that's bad for business. It's a sign that you need to add an employee so you can spend more time keeping your customers happy.

4. Do you feel overwhelmed by your workload? Do you look forward to your work every day, or do you dread it? When you're stressed or unhappy about your work, it shows, and your customers will sense it. When you love your work, it shows, and a smile on your face sends a huge positive signal to your customers.

5. Do you have a life outside your work? When you neglect your personal life because you're working all the time, guess who suffers? Your family and friends. If this describes you, it may be time to add and employee and get your "real" life back!

6. You want to grow your business, but you never seem to have time to pursue new opportunities or plan your business future. Hiring an employee can give you that vital time to plan for your bigger and better home watch business.

If you found yourself saying "yes" to one or more of these six reasons, read on while we cover the right way to find and hire your first new employee.

How To Find Good Employees

Start with a job description. To attract the right applicants, you need to write a simple job description. Focus on education, experience and "soft skills," such as a "people person" ability to organize and time management.

A G.E.D. or a high school diploma is a reasonable minimum requirement, as nursery work requires the ability to read and write at a basic level. Also, I've found new hires with a recent military background to be excellent employees, as the military service has trained them to be punctual, courteous and eager to succeed in the civilian world.

Older folks in their 50s and 60s can also be capable employees, especially if your working schedule is flexible. New hires with previous nursery or landscaping experience can be great hires, and they have proven their ability to do the work with another employer.

Pre - Hiring Setup

Background Checks. A pre-employment background check is recommended for all new hires. Better to get any bad news before you hire than after. What information you can check on depends on your state regulations, but almost all states allow a criminal background check and a drug test, the two most important checks for you to consider.

To order a background check, do a web search for "criminal background check in (your state)" Compare prices from at least 3 providers before you order a check.

The U.S. Equal Employment Opportunity Commission has strict rules that must be followed if you do a background check. You must notify the applicant in writing that you intend to order a background check. In addition, the applicant must provide a signed consent to the check. If you are ordering a credit check, the same rules apply, plus you must notify the applicant if you refuse to offer the applicant a job because of information in the credit report.

Drug testing is often included in a complete background check, especially because of the nature of this work. Just imagine for a moment what could happen if a person employed by you was involved in a serious accident while out picking up supplies or delivering plants to a contractor's jobsite and was found to be driving under the influence of illegal drugs!

Your insurance company would drop your coverage, those injured could sue you and your business could go bankrupt. So just do it! According to the current federal regulations, an applicant can refuse to take a drug test, but if they do, you probably don't want to hire them, anyway.

The U.S. Civil Rights Act makes it illegal to ask about age, race, ethnicity, color, sex, religion, national origin, disabilities, marital status or pregnancy, whether in a background check, an interview or on a written application.

Advertise Your Job

Once you're prepared, it's time to get the word out. Almost all jobs are listed on online job boards. Explore several to see which one might be the best for your employee search.

Here's a list of the larger national job boards:

- Indeed.com
- Careerbuilder.com
- Craigslist.org
- linkedin.com
- Monster.com
- glassdoor.com
- simplyhired.com
- seek.com

Employee Record Keeping and Taxes

First job - insure your new employees. When you hire employees, you must add worker's compensation insurance. This insurance is required in all states and covers injury or illness while on the job.

For an example, if you hired a new nursery helper who injured their back or slips on an icy sidewalk on the job, worker's compensation insurance pays for their medical care and wages while they are unwilling to work.

In most states, worker's compensation insurance is available through private insurance companies. Only four states, Ohio, North Dakota, Washington and Wyoming, have their own state-run insurance plans.

If you're in one of the other 46 states, contact your current insurance agent or insurance broker to set up this insurance. Your agent can also add a new employee to your surety bond.

Why Hire A Bookkeeper?

When you add employees, the quantity and complexity of record-keeping can be overwhelming. Don't make the mistake of trying to do everything yourself. Your focus should be on running and growing your nursery business.

Few small business owners have the in-depth knowledge of accounts receivable, accounts payable and taxes, and the yearly changes in tax laws and regulations. It's better to hire a professional who has the training and skills to handle this part of your business.

It's also a form of insurance, as missing a bill or a tax filing could affect your business credit rating or result in substantial fees or tax penalties from your state or the I.R.S.

Be sure to hire a bookkeeper that can handle both taxes and payroll so they can handle estimated tax payments, 1099s for independent contractors, Form 940 employment tax forms, W-2 forms and give you a schedule of what is due and when. Unless you enjoy handling these details daily, do yourself a favor and hire a pro!

Never forget, your time is money that can be used towards running your new nursery business and taking it to the next level. A good bookkeeper can save you money by ensuring that you don't make costly accounting mistakes, forget to file a form or a tax payment or forget to send reminders when a customer forgets to pay their bill on time.

If you are on a tight budget, you can use one of the bookkeeping software programs covered earlier to handle the more routine tasks, then transfer the data to a pro for the rest. Quicken, for example, is widely used by bookkeepers and accountants, so sharing date with your bookkeeper is almost seamless.

Save On Taxes

Be sure to keep track of all your business-related expenses, as they may be deductible at tax time. Top deductions include:

- **Vehicle expenses.** At the current 58 cents per mile, this is a big deduction for many nursery businesses.

- **Startup expenses**. The cost of getting your nursery business started is usually deductible. Check with a tax guide or tax professional to get specific deductions.

- **Education expenses.** If you take classes or workshops to maintain or improve your business and professional skills, they may be deductible.

- **Professional fees.** Fees paid to accountants, tax professionals, lawyers, or other professional consultants are deductible.

- **Equipment.** Check with a tax pro to see if there are any special "stimulus" deductions available for the purchase of capital equipment such as vehicles and computers.

- **Interest.** If you use credit to finance business purchases, the interest is deductible.

- **Advertising.** Any marketing costs, such as a magnetic sign for your vehicle or promotional costs, such as sponsoring a little league team or buying equipment for them, is deductible. An excellent book on the subject is *Deduct It—Lower Your Small Business Taxes,* available at www.nolo.com.

What to Pay Your Employees

To find good employees, you will need to pay competitive wages. If nursery workers in your area are making $18 an hour, you need to match that, or finding the best employees will be difficult.

To get started, go to the help-wanted job boards listed earlier and note hourly wages for a home checker in your town. Jot down 10 posted rates, then divide by 10 and you've got the magic number you need to match.

While you're checking the job boards, also study the job descriptions. This will help you write an effective ad or post at the job boards. Some job boards, like Indeed, have a template you can use by simple filling in the blanks for important items like job title, start date, pay rate and required background checks.

CHAPTER 14

Resources

Grower Supplies

A.M. Leonard is one of the largest and oldest suppliers of tools and supplies for pro growers. www.amleo.com.

Dripworks is one of the best sources for drip irrigation supplies and misting systems. One of their pros can help you put together a system that fits your needs, at very affordable prices. www.dripworksusa.com.

Peaceful Valley Farm Supply has an excellent selection or grower supplies, including organic and natural fertilizers and natural pest controls. www.groworganic.com.

Nursery Supplies This company produces a wide variety of plastic nursery containers. You can use their site to find what you're looking for, then a stocking distributor in your area. www.nurserysupplies.com.

B & T Grower Supply. www.growersupply.com. Wholesale nursery supplies, including pots in all sizes, labels, greenhouse supplies and the Pantera oval planters for windowsill herb mini-gardens.

Greenhouse Mega Store. www.greenhousemegastore.com. Wholesale nursery supplies, with a wide range of pots, greenhouse and nursery supplies.

Johnny's Seeds. www.johnnyseeds.com. Growing supplies, wooden plant labels, drip irrigation supplies and specialized hand tools. Best of all, they have developed a system for building affordable "hoop houses" and a "quick hoops" bending tool to make them. Click on their "grower's library" and watch the "quick hoops bender" how-to video. Using quick hoops, you can build both "high tunnel" and "low tunnel" units in a variety of widths and in any length you need.

Wholesale Landscaping Plants

To find nearby sources of seeds, seedlings and container plants, do an online search for "wholesale plant buyer's guide." You'll find plenty of wholesale sources, as each state nursery association maintains a searchable website of member-growers and the plant varieties they specialize in. Two fine examples of this are: **www.nurseryguide.com**, for Oregon-grown plants and **www.tnla.com/buyerguide.php** for Tennessee-grown plants.

www.bloomingnursery.com Excellent selection of potted liners and bare root plants in groundcovers and ornamental grasses.

www.briggsnursery.com Wholesale nursery with a broad range of plant material. They are tissue culture specialists, and have many unusual varieties of plants.

www.midwestgroundcovers.com This family-run nursery has specialized in groundcovers for over 25 years, and has a wide selection of plants.

www.heritageseedlings.com Over 200 varieties of unusual deciduous woody ornamentals to choose from.

www.kurtbluemel.com This grower is one of the pioneers in ornamental grasses, and has one of the best selections available.

www.peekskillnurseries.com A specialty nursery, growing groundcovers only.

Flower Grower Resources

The Flower Farmer, by Lynn Byczynski. If you're just getting started in growing flowers for market, this may be the only book you need! It's a complete guide to growing, post-harvest handling, flower marketing, profiles of successful growers, and detailed production and harvesting information for 100 species of flowers. Available from Amazon.com

Magazines & Newsletters

Growing for Market ... A monthly newsletter for small-scale growers, chock-full of usable, practical ideas, tips and grower profiles. Available from: www.growingformarket.com.

Association of Specialty Cut Flower Growers is an organization of commercial flower growers, with conferences, trade shows, and a bimonthly newsletter. Available from: www.ascfg.org.

Flower Bulbs, Plants & Seeds

Ball Seed Company   www.ballseed.com

W. Atlee Burpee   www.burpee.com

DeVroomen Holland Gardens   www.devroomen.com

Germania Seed Company   www.germaniaseed.com

Fred C. Gloeckner & Co.   www.fredgloeckner.com

G.S. Grimes Seeds   www.grimesseeds.com

Harris Seeds   www.harrisseeds.com

Headstart Nurseries   www.headstartnursery.com

Horticultural Products & Services   www.hpsseed.com

Johnny's Selected Seeds. Best source for new growers, with smaller seed packs for smaller gardens. www.johnnyseeds.com

Park Seed Company   www.parkseed.com

Stokes Seeds   www.stokesseeds.com

Herb Seeds

Richter's Herbs. www.richters.com. Herb specialists that can supply not only seed for hundreds of herbs, but growing information and books on commercial scale herb production and processing.

Johnny's Seeds. www.johnnyseeds.com. Seeds for the small-scale commercial herb grower, as well as growing supplies, wooden plant labels, drip irrigation supplies and specialized hand tools.

First, thank you for purchasing and reading this book. I hope it has provided both the resources and the motivation for you to start your own backyard plant nursery. Starting your own small business is the ticket to a better life and a prosperous future, and freedom from worries about job security.

If you have a moment, I'd really love a review. Reviews are a huge help to authors, myself included. If you enjoyed this book, please take a minute or two to post a review on Amazon. Just enter the title of this book at Amazon.com, then click on "reviews," then "write a review. Thanks so much for your support!

Wishing you much success in your new business,

Made in United States
North Haven, CT
26 July 2022

21847055R00114